4 WEEKS

GETTING STARTED IN PROBLEM SOLVING AND MATH CONTESTS

GETTING STARTED

IN

MICHAEL W. ECKER

PROBLEM

SOLVING

AND

Franklin Watts / 1987
New York / London
Toronto / Sydney

MATH

CONTESTS

The AJHSME, AHSME, and AIME sample exams and
sample exam questions are used with the permission
of the Committee on the American Mathematics
Competitions, © The Mathematical Association of
America. The sample Gauss Division problems are used
with permission from The Canadian Mathematics
Competition, University of Waterloo, Waterloo, Ont.

Diagrams by Vantage Art

Library of Congress Cataloging-in-Publication Data

Ecker, Michael W.
Getting started in problem solving and math contests.

Bibliography: p.
Includes index.
Summary: Presents mathematical problem-solving skills
useful for examinations and contests, including trial
and error, searching for patterns, shortcuts, and
changing perspective.
1. Problem solving—Juvenile literature.
[1. Problem solving. 2. Mathematics] I. Title.
QA63.E25 1987   153.4'3   86-26790
ISBN 0-531-10342-0

ACKNOWLEDGMENTS

Thanks to all the problem-solving giants who preceded me, making this book easier to write.

Thanks to my editor, Henry Rasof, for his encouragement and professional help.

Thanks mostly to my wife, Susan; my children, Melody and David; and all my family and friends. I dedicate this book to them, in appreciation of their forbearance during those times I had to be busy writing instead of giving them the love and attention they deserve.

CONTENTS

GETTING STARTED IN PROBLEM SOLVING AND MATH CONTESTS

PREFACE

Will This Book Make You an Expert?

In a word, No, this book can't make you an expert on problem solving or math competitions. I can't make you an expert. Teachers can't, either.

Only you can do this.

But this book and teachers can help. Maybe we won't make you into an expert, but we can improve your skills in mathematical thinking, whether to participate in math contesting, or just to learn to think at a deeper level.

Such skills carry to other parts of one's life. Problem solving sharpens critical thinking and makes us more aware. It is also an integral part of many professions as well: not just mathematics but all the sciences, criminology, medicine, law—virtually all activities in which human creativity is involved.

One additional bonus is that some of the problem skills we'll consider can help you with other exams, most notably entrance-type exams such as the SAT (often required for college entrance) and the GRE (an analogous exam for entrance to graduate schools). I've found that there is sufficient overlap of certain ideas to merit their inclusion.

In writing this book, I have deliberately focused on as many of the most frequently used problem-solving skills as I have been able to identify in my own activities not just as a mathematician, teacher, professor and problem solver but also as a computerist and writer. Since the topic called mathematics is so gargantuan, it is impossible to cover every possibility. I do hope readers will touch bases with other books as well, asking teachers to direct them to the works of such notables as Polya, a twentieth-century legend in this area.

More to the point, I hope that readers understand that no book will cover all the actual mathematical topics needed for the various exams, contests, and competitions which they may enter. I have, however, incorporated some of the best tips and tricks which have universal appeal, as found in many different exams.

Since there are occasional tendencies towards mathematical recreations in mathematics competitions, and since this is an area of personal interest, one which has the capacity to interest you more in mathematics, I have included a few tidbits from recreational mathematics as well.

What Is the Goal of This Book?

I present those ideas useful for solving problems, whether for exams or other use, which are most overlooked in schools: trial and error, generalization via searching for patterns, limitations of patterns, shortcuts, changing perspective, and so on. Too much of the time we in the "math establishment" offer pat answers and pat solutions. Life and mathematics are both complex and creative.

What's so terrible about dealing with some of that complexity and creativity?

So, this book is no substitute for learning mathematics but rather is intended as a supplement to beef up your problem-solving "how-to" knowledge.

As a problem solver myself, I use these techniques, and commend them to you. I hope that you find them as helpful as I have.

I invite suggestions, comments, and discussion, as problem solving remains an ongoing interest. Write me directly: Dr. Michael W. Ecker, 129 Carol Drive, Clarks Summit, PA 18411.

1

ARE MATH, PROBLEM SOLVING, AND CONTESTS FOR ME?

This book will tell you what it's like to get involved with math contests. What are they? How do I enter? Can I learn the tricks and numerous problem-solving techniques to do better—or even win?

Before we go into these, it is important to dispel a common but mistaken notion, namely, the idea that you have to be a mathematical genius to get involved in math contests.

Just as many people enjoy sports and some participate competitively, so can people get involved with contests of the mind, and particularly of the mathematical mind. Instead of brawn against brawn, it's brain against brain. It may be true that being a mathematical genius helps a lot, but there are not that many geniuses around. Many students get involved anyway.

What does it take? The fundamental prerequisites are a curiosity about things and relationships. You also should have a desire and willingness to learn more. If you already know that you enjoy mathematics or do well in it, then you are, of course, a prime candidate for a math contester.

It makes little sense to insist that one be "good" in mathematics, as though being good in math is a genetic condition limited to a few. Some people do have a greater inclination toward mathematics. Still, for the most part, learning and enjoying mathematics depend more on education, practice, encouragement from family, and so on.

The situation is much as with sports. Some people have bodies that are inherently more athletic. However, the way they exercise and train those bodies plays a critical role in their future success as athletes. Likewise, how well you may do mathematically depends on the mental pushups, pullups, and situps you do, with your success as a "mathlete" being the final measure for you.

To get you to see whether you might enjoy the stimulation of problem solving and math contesting, I have prepared a few favorite brain-teasers and math recreations. While not all contests have such interesting questions, we often find that some of the best math students are attracted to math because of interesting recreations such as these. There is no time limit to these, and you should play with whichever questions you wish. Answers, solutions, and comments will appear at the back of the book for this and succeeding chapters.

Enjoy! I'll rejoin you next chapter, where we will look more closely at the "nuts and bolts" of contests.

Sample Brainteasers

1. Do you know Roman numerals? Then consider that system's nine, or IX, as it stands. Challenge: Without erasing anything and just by adding one symbol, can you convert IX into the numerical equivalent of the number 6?

2. Figure 1 contains eight little boxes or squares of the same size. This is your mission, should you decide to accept it: Place each of the digits 1, 2, 3, 4, 5, 6, 7, 8 in the eight boxes, with a different digit in each small box, so that boxes that are touching horizontally, vertically,

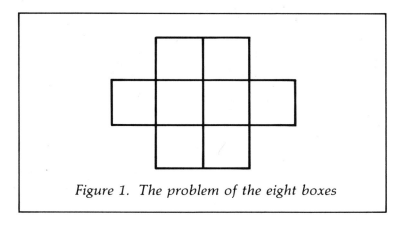

Figure 1. The problem of the eight boxes

or even diagonally, do not contain adjacent numbers (such as 3 and 4).

3. A lake has a top view in the shape of a square. At each corner of the square is a tree. You wish to enlarge the lake so that the top view is now that of a square with exactly twice the area of the original square. Yet, you don't want any of the trees to be surrounded by water; nor may you move any trees. How is this possible? (Hint: Draw the lake. Now what?)

4. You have six glasses, three filled with water and three empty, as shown in Figure 2. Touching only one glass, how can you arrange it so that the filled and empty glasses alternate (full, empty, full, empty, full, empty)?

Figure 2. The problem of the six glasses

2

WHAT ARE
MATH CONTESTS
ALL ABOUT?

Now that we've settled the question of whether math contesting is something which might be of some interest to you, let's return to a more basic question: What is this all about, anyway? In other words, what are contests like? Are there prizes? How can you train for one? Should you guess if you don't know the answer to a particular question? How do you get involved? Does it hurt? Is it fun? And so forth.

As with so many other things in life, mathematics competitions come in many guises. There is no such thing as a standard exam. Some last one hour; others, more prestigious, could require four hours.

Although some are called "contests" instead of something else, none of these should be confused with a lottery, sweepstakes, or random drawing to win money, cars, or trips. In each case, you are competing against others in your solving of preselected math problems.

Almost all contests have you go to a specific location set aside on a specific date and time. You bring with you pencils and other materials as instructed by a teacher, or by an instruction booklet which you receive ahead of time. Make sure you pay careful attention to these instructions!

Unless you're involved in a team competition, you will be working alone; it's somewhat as in taking a regular test. You will have a definite time limit in which to complete as many problems as you can, with all contestants starting and finishing at the same time. Most contests offer scratch paper, and some have a separate form on which you record your final answers, especially if the test is computer-scored. In those, be sure to record answers carefuly and clearly, avoiding stray marks or writing too lightly.

Only the most competitive and prestigious involve essay questions, proofs, and detailed discussion.

Sample Exams

Let me give you some idea of the extremes, and you'll get the idea.

On one end, there are the many small school, local, and regional exams. These tend to be of varying quality. Some appear to have been so hastily composed that they are replete with numerous spelling errors! Most are quite good, however. This area is a good one in which to get started. Competition will not be so keen, and the questions won't be as demanding. Typically, the questions are drawn from class material you've had in the past two years or so. Most are at the high school level, although quite a few are at the junior high and college levels now, too.

In the middle, one typical exam is at the junior college level: the American Mathematical Association of Two-Year Colleges' (AMATYC) Student Mathematics League Contest. Many or most of the questions are accessible even to well-prepared high school students with a background up to precalculus. Another one is the AHSME, about which more will be said below.

At the high end are the national and international olympiads. Most of these "high end" competitions are for high-schoolers, although some biggies such as the Putnam identify the best college-level students.

Whether at the junior college level, as with this

AMATYC event, or at the junior or senior high level, the primary reward is recognition. Most contests offer some additional tangible rewards: certificates to all achieving a certain score; pins and medals indicating first, second, third places and honorable-mention; as well as plaques, books, and even free one-year memberships in math-related organizations.

In a recent and encouraging development, we've begun to witness increased support of math contesting and the winners at all levels. For instance, in some states, such as Pennsylvania and Ohio, some colleges are offering fixed cash scholarships to winners who choose to attend those schools. With the clamor for more support of mathematics and mathematics teaching, expect to see more substantial scholarships offered by more schools. We hope this trend continues.

Exams of the Committee on American Mathematics Competitions

Most exams are carefully planned and crafted. Consider the Committee on American Mathematics Competitions (CAMC), for instance, outlined in the chart.

The CAMC is the overseeing committee for four exams taken annually by half a million students or more, most of them in the United States. Within the CAMC and its subcommittees which actually write the exams, selection of problems is a painstaking process involving many levels of review, concern for balance, level, and so on.

After selection of problems created by the committee members, these same members try to offer the best, most elegant solutions. That is, they try to write up the best way to arrive at the final answer in each case. This is to ensure that, when the students get to see the solutions later on, they get not only the correct results, but see at least one good method for handling the question.

Contests of the Committee on American Mathematics Competitions

	AJHSME	AHSME	AIME	USAMO
open to/ taken by	junior high students	high school students	high school students who meet AHSME cutoff (invitation only)	the best high school students (AIME & AHSME scores used to select)
number of students involved (annually)	175,000– 250,000	350,000– 500,000	500– 2,000	50–100
answer format	multiple choice	multiple choice	integers 0–999	essay (open style)
typical number of questions	25	30	15	5
difficulty level	moderate	moderate	intermediate	difficult
time limit	40 min.	1½ hr.	3 hr.	4 hr.

This includes close scrutiny of the language used, right down to correct placement of spaces and commas. Such is the dedication here to produce exams which are not only correct, but also educational, good examples, and even fun.

The CAMC is sponsored by the Mathematical Association of America (MAA), the National Council of Teachers of Mathematics (NCTM), and several other national mathematics-related organizations. The CAMC's four exams are, in order of increasing difficulty and/or level: the American Junior High School Mathematics Examination (AJHSME), the newest one; the American High School Mathematics Examination (AHSME), also known as the Annual High School Mathematics Examination; the American Invitation Mathematics Examination (AIME); and the prestigious USA Mathematical Olympiad (USAMO).

The AHSME is an exam taken each year by about four hundred thousand to half a million high school students in the United States and around the world. The exam is of the multiple-choice variety, with thirty questions drawn from traditional areas of high school mathematics (algebra, geometry, trigonometry, etc.). These have to be answered in an hour and a half. Each question has five choices for answers. Of course, since one purpose is to identify mathematical talent, the questions are not all routine, and some require creativity.

The AJHSME may be thought of as a kind of AHSME for junior high students. Its purpose is similar as well, but the idea is to encourage problem solving and identify mathematical talent at an earlier age, as well as to provide a competitive focus for talented, budding, or potential mathematicians at the junior high level. Sample questions appear in Chapter 12.

The AIME was created in the early 1980s as an intermediate exam with the explicit goal of offering another level of recognition and encouragement for students, as well as to help select participants for the hardest of the four competitions, the Olympiad (USAMO). Prior to that, the best scorers on the AHSME were the invitees for the Olympiad. Now, the best scorers on the AHSME (usually about one thousand to two thousand students) are invited to take the AIME. In turn, the best AIME scorers are invited to take the USAMO. In some cases, however, a very high score on the AHSME may qualify a student for the Olympiad. On the AIME subcommittee, we have used this alternative to get a desirable number of contestants for the Olympiad, that number being between fifty and one hundred.

One striking difference between the AIME and the AHSME is in the formats. Unlike the latter, the AIME is a fifteen-question, three-hour exam (previously two and a half hours, but recently changed) in which each answer is an integer from 000 to 999, inclusive. This often creates special demands on the constructors of this exam to accommodate this format. The primary purpose of this is to allow simple computer-scoring in Lincoln, Nebraska, where the executive director is based, as well as to allow more choices than the five choices of the AHSME.

Having more choices, you realize, decreases the guessability of answers. If it's any small consolation to you, there is no penalty for guessing here. But note that creativity, mathematical knowledge, and talent, now at a much greater premium, are more significant at this level.

For the USAMO, the demands are the harshest, the secrecy behind the exam the greatest. The questions are virtually essay-level at this stage, and many professors of mathematics with PhD's confess to having difficulty with the problems. The time limit is around four hours, and each paper is scored carefully and meticulously to find subtle elements of mathematical sophistication and elegance. As a further indication of the care, secrecy, and importance at this level, consider this: even some members of the USAMO subcommittee itself have not been privy to the final selection of exam questions until the exam itself!

For all these exams, the greater the prestige of the exam, the greater the rewards in terms of recognition. Material rewards, however, are not that much greater than with the smaller exams, except for the scholarships sometimes offered to the top winners.

Other Exams

Nevertheless, bear in mind that most other exams are not designed for selection of the best in the country or the best in the world. The majority of exams are geared toward the regional, local, and even school levels, and there is plenty of room for participation, and that means for you, too. You'll see examples of these at the end of Chapter 12.

In view of the diversity available, it is impossible to generalize about such matters of advice as whether or not to guess. This is something which you must find out about long before the contest. The same applies to methods of scoring. Some exams have clearly spelled out scoring formulas which give you the clue as to this, such as: number of points = 5 times number right, minus 2 times number wrong, minus number blank.

One ramification of this sample scoring formula would be that there is a greater penalty for wild guessing than leaving an answer blank. This is typical of some of the exams. If you can eliminate some choices, however, guessing is worthwhile. Many have no penalty for blanks, however, so again, know the details of scoring, time limits, etc., before the exam.

One word of caution: Math competitions and the scores awarded are not comparable in any way to scores on conventional exams. For instance, a score of 15 out of a possible 25 on the AJHSME might tempt you to conclude that you did poorly, because $15/25 = 3/5 = 60\%$. *Do not* succumb to this kind of thinking! If you do, you'll only make yourself feel bad! There is no basis for comparision with standard exams in schools. In point of fact, 15 out of 25 on the AJHSME would probably be regarded as better than average in any case!

How Do I Get Started?

The place to start is with your school, and most likely, your math teacher. Ask him or her which exams the school itself offers or administers for organizations such as the CAMC. If your teacher doesn't know (and many don't, unfortunately), speak to other math teachers or the department chairman. You should find that your teachers and your school will be delighted to help you and to offer you encouragement. If there is a math club or math team, find out how to get involved.

Remember to learn all you can about the types of questions asked, the material you will need to concentrate on, how the scoring is done, whether to guess, when and where the competition will be offered, what to bring, and so on. You'll have to work on such elements as watching and allocating time, too. Of course, continue learning all you can, and bone up on those special skills!

This book is designed to help sharpen your skills, and contesting itself can help, too. Unlike exams which you need for your courses or which are administered to enter college, math competitions are voluntary. Still, the idea of taking a test that you don't have to may be scary to you. But remember: You will not be getting a course grade from the kind of competition we are talking about. Few people will know how you did, unless you decide to tell them. Your getting into college or graduate school, or your getting a job or starting a career, cannot be hurt. In other words, while doing well can bring pride, attention, and acclaim, you can't lose, for results are confidential. Contests have fewer winners than non-winners, and nobody automatically expects you to win. Even if you don't win the contest, you still are a winner for what you accomplish. There are later contests, if you wish, as well as opportunities to improve.

Let's begin our look, then, into solving problems.

3 SEARCHING FOR PATTERNS

Problem solving is the central theme of all math contests and of mathematics itself, perhaps the only common thread of math contests. This chapter deals with a first important technique: the use of patterns. Consider the following:

1. Suppose that I asked you to tell me which natural number (1, 2, 3, 4, . . .) is the 450th odd number. Could you determine it?

2. Recall that positive-integer exponents, or powers, are defined as follows: $a^1 = a$, $a^2 = a \times a$, $a^3 = a \times a \times a$, etc.

    A. How many multiplication signs are there in writing down a^{1003}?

    B. More to the point, what is the units digit (the rightmost digit) in the final result of raising 3 to the 1003rd power?

Both questions have one feature in common: They involve large numbers. Hence, we need a strategy, one which works well in cases where there is some kind of regularity or pattern, as in these. Let's try working with smaller numbers to see whether we can find a pattern. If we find one, we can try to apply it to our original question.

Solution to 1. It is unfeasible to write down the first 450 odd numbers. Instead, our plan is to see that there are several patterns for getting the nth odd number—in other words, a formula for any particular odd number. From the formula, we'll then compute the 450th odd number.

One formula that many people see is that each number is expressible in the form of 1 + an even number. So, the question is reduced to an easier one, namely, working with even numbers. Note the supplementary role of reducing the problem to something more familiar. With it, we can now begin to develop a pattern, as in this chart:

$$
\begin{aligned}
1 &= 1 + 0 \\
3 &= 1 + 2 \\
5 &= 1 + 4 \\
7 &= 1 + 6 \\
9 &= 1 + 8 \\
&\text{etc.}
\end{aligned}
$$

This is better, but we still need to take this further. Suppose we now note that we can break this down more by writing:

$$
\begin{aligned}
1 &= 1 + 0 \times 2 \\
3 &= 1 + 1 \times 2 \\
5 &= 1 + 2 \times 2 \\
7 &= 1 + 3 \times 2 \\
9 &= 1 + 4 \times 2
\end{aligned}
$$

Now extend this even further by noting that we are interested in developing a relationship between which numbered term of the sequence we are dealing with— such as the first, second, third—and the actual odd number itself, such as 1, 3, 5, ... We then note:

Term Number	Term Itself
1	$1 = 1 + 0 \times 2$
2	$3 = 1 + 1 \times 2$
3	$5 = 1 + 2 \times 2$
4	$7 = 1 + 3 \times 2$
5	$9 = 1 + 4 \times 2$

and so on. Note the pattern, which is now clear. The nth term is $1 + (n-1) \times 2$, or $1 +$ the result of (1 less than n) times 2.

That example illustrates this approach for dealing with large numbers:

1. Use appropriate smaller values.
2. Rewrite, if necessary, to discern a pattern or formula.
3. Apply the general pattern you just found to your large number.

If we apply this to the example we just considerd, we apply our pattern to $n = 450$ to find that the 450th odd number should be $1 + 449 \times 2 = 1 + 898$ (remember that we multiply before we add in the absence of grouping symbols), or 899.

In some situations, just the general formula of step 2 is required, as in the question of finding a formula for the nth odd number or the sum of the first n even numbers. However, whether there is a specific large number or just the general formula, there remains the last question: How do we know whether the pattern really persists? Is it possible that the pattern breaks down, invalidating the formula? Suffice it to say that this is a concern, although it is not the case here. We will not concern ourselves with this right now.

Note that the above solution to item 1 could have

been handled a bit more simply by thinking of each odd number as 1 less than an even number, rather than 1 more. That is, think of 1 as 1 less than 2, 3 as 1 less than 4, 5 as 1 less than 6, etc. This would lead to the result that the nth odd number is 1 less than the nth even number, or 1 less than 2n (i.e., 2 times n). So, we get $2n-1$ as the nth odd number. The previous result we had was $1 + 2(n-1)$ above, but this equals $1 + 2n - 2$, or $2n-1$. Hence, there is more than one way to arrive at a pattern even in such a simple case as this one.

Solution to 2. For part A, if we look at the second power, third power, and so on, we can see that the number of multiplication signs is always 1 less than the power. When we have a second power, there is only one multiplication involved; for a third power, there are two multiplications. Since this is a clear pattern, for the 1003rd power, the answer is 1002 (not 1003).

For part B, you probably realize that, as with question 1, it is almost crazy to try to calculate such a large quantity as the number 3 to the power 1003. Instead we note a pattern from the "cyclic" behavior of the result of 3 raised to various powers:

power	result	units digit
1	3	3
2	9	9
3	27	7
4	81	1
5	243	3
6	729	9

Note the beginning of a pattern: 3, 9, 7, 1; 3, 9, 7, 1, etc., always repeating in cycles of four. In view of this cycle involving four answers, we realize that the question boils down to throwing away all the multiples of 4 in 1003. In other words, the remainder is crucial here.

Okay, let's divide 1003 by 4.

Since the remainder in the process of this division is 3 (the partial quotient is 250 but is not needed), we realize that the rightmost digit, or units digit, of 3 to the 1003rd power, will be the same as if we had just raised 3 to the third power. Hence, the answer is 7, completing our solution to the second question.

The Jailer Problem

The foregoing method of looking for a pattern can even be applied to complex-sounding problems. Here's a gem from recreational mathematics, but it's a bit involved. It features an oddball warden who plays games with prisoners in prison cells.

Imagine a jail with 100 prisoners and 100 closed cells, consecutively numbered 1, 2, . . . , 100, with one convict per cell. One day, the warden announces an unusual mathematical scheme to determine the beneficiaries of a partial amnesty. Certain cells will be opened, others closed, and others unaffected at each minute of the next 100 minutes of time. At the end of the 100 minutes, any convict in an open cell may leave. (None may leave, however, during the intermediate phase.) The question is to determinine who will go free at the end. Will number 81? How about number 99? Number 100?

Let's refer to the open versus closed condition of the cell as its condition. Our warden now carries out the following action over the course of the 100 minutes. At minute 1, he reverses every cell's condition, so all are now open. At minute 2, he reverses every *second* cell's condition, so cells numbered 2, 4, 6, . . . , 100 are now closed. At minute 3, he reverses every *third* one, and so on, until the 100 minutes have elapsed.

In general, for each number k = 1, 2, . . . , 100, at minute k, the warden reverses the condition—the openness or closedness—of each kth cell. To reiterate the offer, any prisoner in a cell open after the 100th minute may go free.

You can see how it starts to become unclear which cells are open at which times. Using some trial-and-error experimentation, let's see what happens to some of the cells. Cell 1 is opened at minute 1. At minute 2, it is not affected, nor is it affected at any later time (as 1 is not an integral multiple of any of 2, 3, . . . , 100). Hence, prisoner number 1 will be freed. Cell 2's occupant is less fortunate: His cell is opened at minute 1, closed at minute 2, and then unaffected at later moments. Note that once the minute number exceeds the cell number, that cell's condition is not changed again. If we continue with cell 3, we have it open at minute 1, unaffected at minute 2, closed at minute 3, so by the observation, cell 3 will remain closed. As our last example, the resident of cell 4 is more fortunate: For minutes 1 through 4, the sequence is open, closed, bypassed, open—never to be touched again—with prisoner 4 therefore being set free. From this, can we generalize without having to handle each case individually, going all the way to 100?

One thing which we might do is make a chart, as in Figure 3. The chart simply keeps track of which cells are open at which moments by use of a numeral 1; a closure is indicated by a 0, and a cell bypassed at a given instant is left blank in the chart. Using diagrams effectively is in itself a valuable skill, too. However, let's just think of it as an aid in our goal: finding a pattern.

Can you see the pattern which is beginning to emerge? Note the diagonal "line" in Figure 3. A cell winds up being open at the end if and only if the cell's number is a perfect square. Assuming that this pattern persists, we can see that since 81 is a perfect square, cell 81 should be one of the open cells. On the other hand, cell 99 shoud turn out to be closed at the end of the 100 minutes, as 99 is not a perfect square.

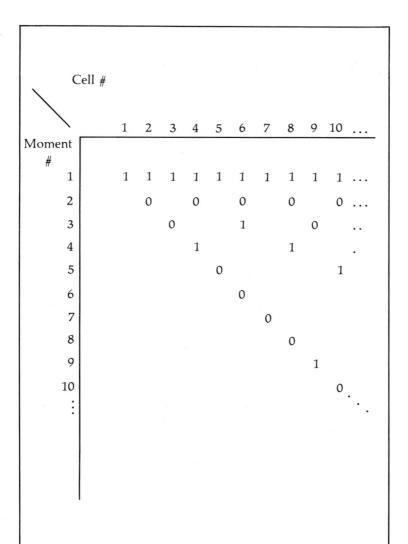

Figure 3. The "eccentric jailer problem" solved. Here, the key is: 1 = open, 0 = closed, blank = unchanged at moment. You can read the final results from the diagonal entries from upper left to lower right.

Patterns may not be the only method we have, as we'll soon see, but they constitute an effective one in situations of some kind of regularity.

Problems and Challenges

1. What is the sum of the first 50 odd numbers?

2. What is the sum of the first 100 even numbers? (Hint: take the sum using only one even number, then only two, then only three. For each of these, note that you can factor each answer—that is, write it as a product—in a certain kind of way which is the same for all the answers.)

3. What is the sum in the following? $1/(1 \times 2) + 1/(2 \times 3) + 1/(3 \times 4) + \ldots + 1/(99 \times 100)$. [Here, the ". . ." indicates that we are saying "and so on" in the process. For instance, even though you don't see the fourth term, it is $1/(4 \times 5)$.]

4. What is the sum in the following? (Do not just add!) $1/2 + 1/4 + 1/8 + 1/16 + \ldots + 1/4096$. (Each denominator is double the previous one, and 4096, or 2 to the 12th power, is the 12th one.)

5. How many squares of all sizes are there on a standard 8×8 checkerboard?

6. A chiliagon is a polygon of 1000 sides. (The prefix is akin to "kilo," meaning thousand.) If you pick any one vertex, how many distinct diagonals, in theory, can be drawn from that vertex to another vertex? How many triangles are formed in the process?

7. In the jailer problem, how many cells would wind up being open at the end of 1000 moments if there are 1000 cells involved under the term given above?

4 WORKING BACKWARD AND BUILDING BRIDGES

The bacteria in a certain colony are found to double in number every month. At the end of the year, there are approximately 100,000,000 of them. How many were there in the middle of the year (i.e., after six months)?

While the above does not represent an extraordinarily difficult question, it does illustrate an idea of this chapter: working backward. It also reinforces that you should not jump to conclusions hastily (50,000,000 is *not* correct).

Many students are indoctrinated with the need to start with what happens "at the beginning" of the action. Thus, some start solving by saying: Let x be the number of bacteria initially, so that 2x is the number at the end of the first month, etc. Some may quibble with this and let x be the number at the end of the first month, so that 2x is the number at the end of the second, etc. While both will work, neither is necessary.

A more direct route, ironically, is working backward. The cue for this is the fact that you are given information dealing with the end and the middle of some process. Why not avoid algebra and variables by saying that at the end of each month, there are twice as many bacteria as in the previous month? Proceeding in reverse, each month there is half the population that there will be next month (as long as our doubling assumption holds). We can work backward and chart:

End of month number	Population is
12	100,000,000
11	50,000,000
10	25,000,000
9	12,500,000
8	6,250,000
7	3,125,000
6	1,562,500

This is not to say that this is the only way or the best way. The point is to illustrate that it is not always necessary to "work forward" in solving problems. Indeed, much of mathematics requires working backward; some would argue, most of it. I would temper that by this mental picture. Think of your given information as one piece of land. Think of what you want to achieve, find, or prove as another piece of land, this one separated from the first by a gulf of water. Your task is to build a bridge joining the two.

To the extent that your bridge connects the two lands, fine. Anything else may or may not add something. Most of the time, any other steps just waste time or are superfluous.

Some Bridges are Faster

Consider this simple illustration from a general test: Given that $6x + 3 = 75$, can you find the value of $2x + 1$? Stop right now and solve this.

Easy, right? Did you get the answer of 25? Okay, if so, how did you get it? Did you first solve for x? If so, why?

Note that there is no need to determine the value of x. Observe that $2x + 1$ is just one-third of $6x + 3$. But $6x + 3 = 75$, so $2x + 1$ is one-third of this 75 as well, or just 25. Do you see what I mean about building a bridge, and anything else being superfluous? We connected the desired 6x + 3 to the given 2x + 1. Problem solving may not always be this direct, but the bridge analogy is a good way to think about the topic. It can help sharpen your focus so that nothing else will get in your way.

"Routine" Problems

What if the situation *does* allow for a conventional solution technique, as in many algebraic word problems?

Typical question (not hard): Village X has a population of 2500 and has its population rise by 125 per year. Village Y has a population of 5300 and sees its population fall by 75 per year. When will the villages have equal populations?

The typical solution steps are:

1. Start with the question. (What am I looking for?) Define your unknown; use a variable. Use a diagram if it helps you to perceive or summarize the situation.

2. What is the central relationship, or relationships, if more than one? What will lead to an equation, a system of equations, an inequality? (At this point, keep it in words.) In other words, what's the main idea about what's going on?

3. Translate into mathematics.

4. Solve. Also check in the original verbal problem. Watch out for extraneous solutions, solutions which fail to make sense physically, etc.

We implicitly trust that the answer will make sense and probably be integral (i.e., a whole number) although there is no logical reason in fact why this need be so in general. We also assume—in effect, we pretend—that populations behave in such a simplistic manner as to rise or fall by a fixed number over a period of years. We can see clearly, however, that there should be exactly one answer, as the smaller population is rising and the larger population is falling.

Following the steps:

1. Let t = the time in years for the populations to equalize.

2. The idea is that after t years, the populations of villages X and Y are equal. We might abbreviate: Pop X = Pop Y after t years. Don't forget to note the t years.

3. Translate into math. What is the population of X after t years? Of Y? This requires some thought. Our previous chapter on patterns should prove of some help here.

After t = 1 year, the population of X is 2500 + 125; resist the temptation to simplify or calculate here! After t = 2 years, it is 2500 + 250. To better see the pattern, leave that as 2500 + 2 × 125. For t = 3, it's 2500 + 3 × 125.

Can you see the pattern now?

After t years, village X has a population of 2500 + t × 125, or, in more customary notation, 2500 + 125t. Similarly, it's 5300 − 75t for village Y.

Hence, our equation is: 2500 + 125t = 5300 − 75t.

4. If we now solve in the usual manner (get all terms with t on one side, all others on the other side), we should find that we get 200t = 2800, so t = 14. This is a reasonable answer, and we can check that after 14 years, X will have a population of 2500 + 14 × 125 = 2500 + 1750 (remember to watch proper order of operations!), or 4250. For Y, it's 5300 − 75 × 14 = 5300 − 1050 = 4250 again, so our answer checks.

Look for Arithmetical Shortcuts

Although the above solution is a perfectly good one, sometimes our bridge may be built more intuitively. Did you notice that you could handle this question by arithmetic alone? Watch how this solution is a bit more streamlined, yet mirrors what goes on in the algebraic version above.

The populations are initially 2800 apart (5300 − 2500 = 2800). Each year, the populations come closer by 200, as the smaller one goes up by 125 while the larger one goes down by 75. That is, the difference between populations decreases by 200 per year. How many years will it take for this process to "use up" the 2800 difference? That's the same as asking how many times 200 goes into 2800; 2800 divided by 200 is 14.

In the end, we do the same work, but the second is more intuitive and quicker. Nevertheless, in more difficult situations, you will find it almost impossible to rely on your "ordinary number sense" and will find the outlined four-step approach to be of great value.

As a variation, be warned that sometimes the construction of the bridge or link may be more subtle. What if the last problem had asked for the number which would be the population of each village when those figures coincided? In that case, it would not be as obvious that you really need to know the time it will take first in order to get the population figure.

The Game of Fifty

Consider one last example, drawn from recreational mathematics, of building a bridge, but this time stressing again the idea of working in reverse. It is called the Game of Fifty.

Suppose that two players, X and Y, are playing a

game in which each takes a turn picking a number from 1 to 6. X goes first. The players keep a tally of their combined running total as they do this. For instance, X may pick 3, so the tally is 3. Then Y may say 5, so the tally is now $3 + 5 = 8$. Then perhaps X says 6, so the tally is now $3 + 5 + 6 = 14$. The object of this game is to be the player who makes the running total hit or achieve the score of 50 at the end of his turn.

What strategy will win? Does X or Y have an advantage? Which player has the natural advantage? In other words, given full knowledge of how to play perfectly, which player can, by appropriate selection of numbers, always force a win?

This question can be rephrased to accommodate various formats. For instance, we might ask, after providing the given information, for the number which X should pick on his first turn to force a win. We could give a multiple choice of answers, as in (A) 1 (B) 2 (C) 3 (D) 4 (E) 5.

At this point, if you've never played or analyzed this game before, you ought to play it with somebody. It will help you understand and appreciate the solution much more if you do so first. (Go ahead; I'll wait for you!)

In practice, when students are taught this game and play it, what typically happens is a trial in which a lot of numbers are picked hurriedly. Then, as the tally mounts and 40 is approached, the players slow down and become more thoughtful and deliberate in their selections. "What should I pick next?" you can almost hear them thinking. Sometimes one or both players realize that it is desirable to have 43 at the end of the turn, for then, no matter what the opponent picks, the player can win. For instance, with 43, if you now say 1, the total is 44 and I can say 6 and win. With 43, if you say 6, the total is 49 and I can say 1 and win. This is the key first insight for a solution.

This insight is not true of 42 or 44. With 42 after

your turn, I can say 1, get 43 as total, and then win, as I just explained. With 44 as your total, I can win with 6. So, 43 really is the critical number here in the game of 50.

After a couple of rounds of this, students see that they should, in effect, play to achieve 43. How to do this is what they concern themselves with. So, they play and plan and plot. They experiment until somebody discovers that the key is now to get 36, for no matter what the opponent picks next, the player achieving 36 can then make the total 43. So, by what we had before, the player achieving 36 can achieve 43 and therefore 50. After a while, the players can see that they are working backward toward a solution. With the pattern of going down 7 each time (50 to 43 to 36, and so on), they eventually trace back to 1.

To summarize the strategy, player X can always force a win going first with 1, and then when his opponent Y replies x, always choosing 7 minus x. This will ensure that the strategic numbers 1, 8, 15, 22, 29, 36, 43, and 50 are achieved at the end of X's turn. This insight is obtained by working backward from the goal.

Thus, in problem solving, we try to build a bridge between given and desired elements. Thinking in reverse sometimes is what does the trick best.

Problems and Challenges

1. Suppose that you play a game analogous to Fifty, but with a target score of 100, and in which each player may choose from 1 to 8. Who has the natural advantage? How does he or she force a win (strategy)?

2. Suppose now that you play for 100 but with each player choosing 1 to 9. Who has the natural advantage here? How does he or she force a win (what's the strategy)?

3. A square has a diagonal of length 60 centimeters. In square centimeters, what is the area of the square?

4. In Figure 4, a rectangle is inscribed in a quarter-circle, with the sides' lengths as shown. What is the area of the region inside the quarter-circle but not within the rectangle?

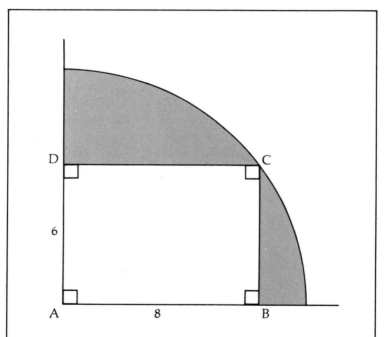

Figure 4. A shaded–area problem in geometry requiring several links in the bridge connecting the given information and the required answer. (AB = 8, AD = 6.)

5. Village A has a population of 1600, which increases by 120 per year; village B has a population of 4200, which decreases by 80 per year. What will be the combined population of the two villages when they have the same number of people in each?

5

UNDERSTANDING THE QUESTION

In the previous chapter, we saw that building a bridge between information provided or known, on the one hand, and what we seek, on the other, are central to problem solving. Sometimes, however, our problem is that we are stuck and don't know how to get started on a problem whose underlying concept is inherently not that difficult.

Consider, for instance, the following three versions of a question, all of which involve the notion of percentage change. Note the differences in ease:

1. What is the percentage increase in price when an item goes from $10 to $12?

2. What is the percentage increase in value in going from 1/2 to 5/8?

3. What is the percentage increase in value in going from $x to $y? (Take y>x.)

Certainly the wording itself is not an issue. Question 1 is unmistakable to anybody who knows how to compute percentage change. Do you get uneasy with the fractions in question 2? Is it just the fractions that cause the problem? The problem might be that you're uncertain of the definition of percentage change. The same is even true with question 3.

My purpose here is not so much to give a lesson on the percentage change concept, an elementary idea, as to use it to exploit two major points:

• It is important to understand definitions fully, clearly, and explicitly. Rote solving of simple cases alone is not sufficient.

• In cases where we are not that clear, we can use analogous questions with easier values to understand better.

Analysis of the Questions

Let's look at these questions individually to see how to apply this. For question 1, most people say they know it's 20%. A typical reply is: "I can just see that the answer is 20%. I don't know how I get it."

With such a response, you're stuck when it comes to questions 2 and 3. So, we must examine question 1 and the answer of 20% more closely if we are to have any hope of answering the question. We see the word "increase" or "change" involved, so we have a cue for subtraction. Aha! We are subtracting! We say $12 - 10 = 2$. Now what? This is to be a percentage change, not an actual change. A percentage of what, though? What does this mean? It means we are seeing what percent of the original amount the change or increase is. What, in turn, does this mean? It means we are seeing what part of the original amount the increase is and we agree to express the resulting fraction as a percent.

So, putting this together, we can say that we are putting the increase, 2, over the original amount, 10, to get $2/10$ or $1/5$. Then we convert the fraction to a percent. This can be done either by converting to a decimal and then to a percent; by familiarity with the fraction involved; by solving a proportion such as $2/10 =$

what/100?; or by multiplying the fraction by 100%. Hence, we do get 20%.

We can make a recipe, as follows:

percentage change = actual change/original amount, result converted to %

(the actual change is the latter value minus the original one)

Having achieved this understanding, we now find that we can solve questions 2 and 3. For question 2, we can say take the difference $5/8 - 1/2 = 5/8 - 4/8 = 1/8$. Now place that over the original amount of $1/2$. Hence, $(1/8)/(1/2) = (1/8) \times (2/1) = 1/4 = 25\%$, the correct answer. You can also do this in other ways which represent slight variations (including using complex fractions and changing to decimals first). The point to reinforce, though, is that lack of clarity is what may hold us back; use of an analogous, simpler problem involving familiar integers instead of fractions or variables may be what will provide the clarity. In a sense, this is a bit like the strategy we used when we worked with smaller numbers in looking for patterns.

We can knock off question 3 easily now with the result we obtained to report the answer as $(y-x)/x$ times 100%, or just $100(y-x)/x$ percent. (The percent sign or word is necessary. Some text authors have become very sloppy and omit it, presumably on the ground that it is understood. It is not, and it must be included. Some exams sometimes test for this with their choices of similar looking answers. Be careful!)

Distance, Rate, Time

Let's take one more example, this one a classic. A car goes from town A to town B at 40 miles per hour average speed, and returns to A from B at an average speed of 60 miles per hour. What is the round-trip average speed?

Setting aside for a moment the question of whether or not the distance between A and B matters (it doesn't), we note the importance of applying the definition correctly. Furthermore, we run into an old nemesis: Don't jump to conclusions; don't just assume that we can say that the average of 40 and 60 is 50, so the answer is 50 miles per hour. This is wrong! The correct answer is actually 48 miles per hour.

To see this, first let's persuade ourselves that 50 is wrong. What is wrong with it? It presumes that you can "average the averages" here. (In fact, this is wrong most of the time.) Why not? In such a trip, you travel for a longer time at the slower speed of 40 than you do at the faster speed of 60. Hence, the average will get "pulled down" below the anticipated 50.

An analogous situation occurs in school grades, bowling scores, and elsewhere. You might have an 88 average for seven semesters of high school, and then get a 92 average for your eighth semester, but your average for all seven semesters will still be under 90.

To return to our car, suppose that the two towns are 120 miles apart. Note the picking of a convenient number for the distance (120 is the least common multiple of 40 and 60); in a later chapter, I'll discuss this point more, but for now, we assume that we are taking a multiple-choice exam with five answer choices (say, 42, 44, 46, 48, 50), so this is fairly safe. Then we invoke the correct definition of average speed, a quantity operationally defined by:

$$\text{average rate} = \text{distance/time, or } r = d/t$$

You can remember this by thinking of the familiar "miles per hour" for speed and noting that "per" indicates a division in mathematics, so a speed is a distance (miles) over (per) time (hour). For our round trip, the total distance is 240 miles. What about the time? Well, it's the sum of the times coming and going. From A to B takes $120/40 = 3$ hours. From B to A takes $120/60 = 2$ hours. The total is 5 hours. Putting the pieces together, we have an average speed of distance/time $= 240/5 = 48$ miles per hour.

Had we wished to avoid using a specific distance, we could have used a variable. We would find later that the variable would "cancel out" anyway and the answer would still be 48. I'll omit this aspect for now.

Finally, note how we have to break the problem down, in the course of building our bridge, to solve the problem. Yet, what I want to remind you of here are several points, some old, some new. (1) Don't jump to hasty conclusions with implicit assumptions which are unjustified. (2) Make sure you know the proper definitions needed for a problem. (3) If you don't, think of an analogous problem, often with simpler numbers and no variables, to help your mind reassemble the correct definition.

Problems and Challenges

1. A small plane flies 100 miles at 400 kilometers per hour, another 100 miles at 300 kilometers per hour, another 100 at 200 kilometers per hour and a last 100 at 100 kilometers per hour. What is the average speed of the plane for this complete trip?

2. What part of 3/4 is 1/10?

3. An item goes on sale and its price is reduced 20%. By what percent would the new price have to be increased in order to restore the original presale price? (A) 15% (B) 20% (C) 25% (D) 33 1/3% (E) not enough information.

4. Tom, Dick, and Mary have a little party. Mary brings five bottles of beverage, Dick brings three, and Tom brings none. The eight bottles have a combined value of $24, and our three partygoers consume equal amounts, finishing all the bottles completely. Later on, Tom feels remorseful about not contributing and says: "Since my share is $8, here's the $8 I owe. You two split it up appropriately." Dick and Mary wish to do this fairly. How much would you advise that each take from the $8?

5. The average of six numbers is 8, and of eight other numbers is 6. What is the average of all these numbers?

6

LISTS, SUMMARIES, AND DIAGRAMS

Sometimes a problem just does not seem to lend itself readily to an easy analysis. How do you get started? There are some things you can do to begin, at least. Perhaps you will then be able to proceed.

By way of example, suppose that you consider United States currency, and wish to know the number of possible combinations of pennies, nickels, and dimes which will make change for a quarter. Most of us begin by forming a list of possibilities. While this is not a particularly advanced technique, it is a useful one. The one thing worth noting is that your list should be *ordered* or *organized* in some fashion. Merely writing down every possible combination in a random fashion will serve to confuse more than to clarify. You won't know whether you've covered every combination, it may be hard to check whether you've done any twice, and you'll take longer, even if you manage to get the correct answer.

Let's use the system of naming the highest-valued coins first, with the next highest following, and so on. This is also known as reverse lexicographical order, since we are really listing in the reverse of a numerical equivalent of alphabetic order. Let's adopt the notation (d,n,p) for the number of dimes, nickels, pennies; for example, (2,1,0) means two dimes, one nickel, and no pennies. Good notation can be not just helpful but also suggestive of solutions.

Our combinations in the notation suggested are then:

(two dimes): (2,1,0); (2,0,5);
(one dime): (1,3,0); (1,2,5); (1,1,10); (1,0,15);
(no dimes): (0,5,0); (0,4,5); (0,3,10); (0,2,15) (0,1,20); (0,0,25).

We now count 2 + 4 + 6 = 12 combinations. Note how the organized manner helped.

We could have handled the same question by using an appropriate diagram. In this case, it, too, would have the virtue of suggesting a counting method. Much as with the organization for the list, we use our ordering scheme to get the tree diagram in Figure 5.

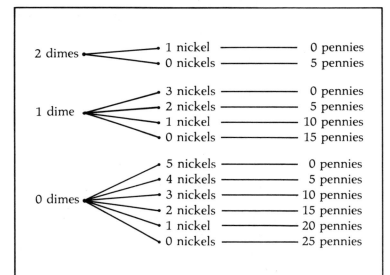

Figure 5. In making change of a quarter, an orderly diagram helps you count the number of ways.

Change for a Dollar, Too

One of the secondary advantages that I claimed for the listing and diagramming methods is their suggestive nature in terms of a solution. For more involved problems, this may be essential. If the problem involves larger numbers, we can also combine what we're doing here with the use of smaller numbers, a technique we considered in the chapter on patterns. What if we had to list all "combos" which provide change for a dollar, instead of a quarter (still using dimes, nickels, pennies only)? How does an organized list or carefully constructed diagram suggest the answer?

We argue, in patternlike fashion, that change of a dollar may be accomplished using a number of dimes equal to 10, or 9, or 8, . . . , or 2, or 1, or 0. For any number of dimes, it then remains to consider the number of nickels, for once we know how many dimes and nickels are picked, the number of pennies is predetermined. For instance, for 8 dimes, you can have 4, 3, 2, 1, or 0 nickels, and in each case, such as 8 dimes and 2 nickels, there is no choice left as to the number of pennies (10 in this particular illustration).

Corresponding to 10 dimes, there is just one choice for nickels, namely, none; for 9 dimes there are three choices for nickels, using 2, 1, or 0; for 8 dimes there are five choices for nickels, namely, 4, 3, 2, 1, or 0; and so on. This leads to a sum of possible numbers of combos equal to $1 + 3 + 5 + 7 + 11 + 13 + 15 + 17 + 19 + 21$, or 121 altogether. In this count, the 1 counted how many combinations used 10 dimes, the 3 counted how many used 9 dimes, all the way to the 21, which counted how many combinations used no dimes (namely, 0 to 20 nickels, or 21 possibilities). As for the answer of 121, note that we don't have to count manually, for we can use patterns to argue that the sum of the first n odd numbers is n^2; hence, it's 121 for these 11.

We did not resort to just a list to answer the case for one dollar. However, by answering the question for a smaller figure (0.25 instead of 1.00), we were able to make a list in an organized fashion and then note a pattern to solve. This technique is frequently useful not just in isolation, but in conjunction with other techniques, notably, looking for patterns.

Counting Routes

Here's another example. In Figure 6, there are two paths indicated going from point A to point B, and four going from point B to point C. Let's call a route from A to C a direct route if it goes through one of the two paths from A to B followed by going through one of the four paths from B to C.

With that in mind, how many direct routes are there from A to C? How would the answer be changed if there

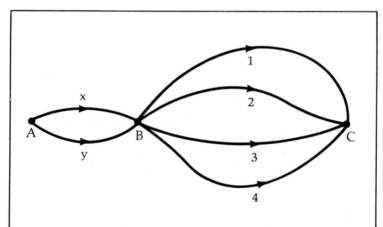

Figure 6. *An illustration of the direct paths from A to C via B*

were twenty paths from A to B and thirty paths from B to C?

As you can see in Figure 7, a simple chart shows the appropriate combinations. There are eight routes for the first question.

You can also see from the little chart that there is a multiplicative principle at work here (the fundamental counting principle), and we've hit upon it by this approach, regardless of whether or not we ever heard of this principle before. Thus, for the second question, there would be 20 × 30 = 600 routes.

Problems and Challenges

1. Count the number of distinct ways to make change for two dollars in U.S. currency if you use just dimes, nickels, and pennies.

	1	2	3	4
x	x,1	x,2	x,3	x,4
y	y,1	y,2	y,3	y,4

Figure 7. The chart shows that there are 2 × 4 = 8 paths from A to C via B in the previous diagram. In the chart, "x,2" represents following x and then 2.

2. Draw a diagram in a suggestive way to represent that the sum of the first ten odd numbers, 1 through 19, is 10 × 10 or 100. (Hint: For 3, use three dots; for 5, five dots, etc. Form a shape suggestive of 10 × 10.)

7

THE DANGER OF IMPLICIT ASSUMPTIONS

In the first chapter, I asked some trick questions. For instance, do you remember the one about forming a numerical equivalent of 6 from the letters IX by just adding one symbol and not erasing anything? If you've checked the answer key at the back of the book, you already know there is a simple answer: SIX. In other words, just place the letter S in front. What made this tricky was the false cue given when you were asked whether you knew Roman numerals. This suggested that I wanted a solution which was itself Roman numeral.

Rather than dwell on whether or not you got it, realize that I never stated that the answer had to be a Roman numeral! You may have *assumed* it, but that is precisely the point: You must guard against making implicit or unconscious assumptions. This means you must be careful not to believe some limitation applies simply because something suggests that such is the case.

Let's examine this further. Although such questions are frequently found among the brain-teaser type of question, the lesson is helpful on exams where creativity and imagination are called for. In the real world, people professionally involved in solving problems (police detectives, researchers, medical examiners, mathematicians) learn this lesson: "It's not so much what we don't know that makes us unable to solve the problem; it's the things we think we know which are wrong."

A Simple Example from Geometry

Consider the line segment PT in Figure 8. Suppose that we know point R to be the midpoint of line segments PT and QS. Which of the following is true? (A) PQ < RS (B) PQ = RS (C) PQ > RS (D) there is not enough information.

Go ahead now and answer the question before reading on.

If you've considered this, you might have been tempted to answer (B) PQ = RS. The diagram is very suggestive of this. But now try to prove this to be so. After a while, you will find that you are unable to prove this. Might you have made a mistake?

Maybe. Redraw Figure 8 to make it like Figure 9 or Figure 10. Do you see that each of these diagrams satisfies the original requirements that R be the midpoint of

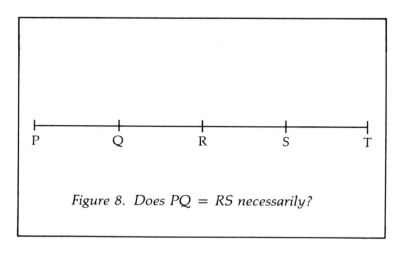

Figure 8. Does PQ = RS necessarily?

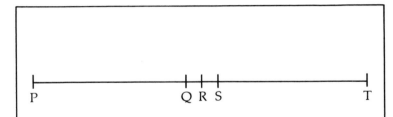

Figure 9. PQ > RS in this diagram. Perhaps this is an equally correct sketch.

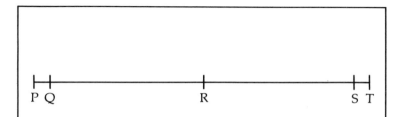

Figure 10. PQ < RS in this diagram. This, too, is a possible picture.

both PT and QS? That is, we still have PR = RT and QR = RS. Hence, Figures 9 and 10 model the given information as well as does Figure 8. Although you may have been tempted to make the implicit assumption that PQ = RS based on the overly suggestive original diagram, you see now that having such a belief is jumping to conclusions.

One antidote to overly suggestive diagrams is to redraw them in different ways. However, you may not change any of the given information. If the above had specified that PQ is 1 centimeter long as well, any new diagram would also have to feature PQ as 1 centimeter long. Seeing the diagram drawn in alternate fashions, as long as they do not contradict the given information, often helps to weed out some things we may accept too quickly without justification.

A Simple Algebraic Example

An analogous question in a more algebraic setting might involve a comparison of $5 + x$ and $5 - x$, with choices: (A) $5 + x$ is larger (B) they're equal, (C) $5 - x$ is larger (D) there is not enough information.

At first glance, you may be tempted to choose (A) and say that $5 + x$ is larger. However, nothing rules out the possibility of x being 0, which would then make the quantities equal. This does not make the answer (B), but it rules out (A). Hence, the answer is (D).

What if we give the same question and stipulate that x is not 0? What is the answer now?

The answer is still not (A), because x could be negative. For instance, with $x = -1$, $5 + x = 4$, whereas $5 - x = 6$, so $5 - x$ can be larger. The answer is still (D).

We see the need to consider all kinds of numbers before jumping to conclusions via implicit assumptions that x is a certain kind of number or numbers. This is similar in strategy to considering different ways the diagram might legitimately look in a geometry problem. It's not easy to combat these tendencies, but we have to try, at least, to be more careful.

Problems and Challenges

1. Find another solution to the problem of adding one symbol to make IX become the numerical equivalent of a 6.

2. You have six matchsticks of equal size. From them, it is desired to form four triangles of the same size, with a matchstick length as the length of each side. How?

3. You are in a room whose shape is that of a cube 15 meters long by 15 meters wide by 15 meters high. The walls are made of solid concrete, there are no windows larger than 10 centimeters by 10 centimeters, and the door is made of titanium, one of the strongest materials in the world. How do you escape?

4. In the problem with the midpoints, suppose we add that PQ is 1 centimeter long, as considered in the discussion of varying the diagram. Does that change the answer to the original question? What if we specify that QR is 2 centimeters long (but do not specify the length of PQ)?

5. If $x < 0$, how do $5 + x^2$ and $5 - x^2$ compare? Do we need the full hypothesis that $x < 0$ to arrive at a conclusion, or can we arrive at a conclusion with less information than that?

8 THE LIMITATIONS OF PATTERNS AND EXAMPLES

Look at the functional expression $f(n) = n^2 - n + 41$, using the values $n = 0, 1, 2, 3, \ldots$ ad infinitum (that is, forever). What can we say about the results? That is, we seek general truths about the function values $f(n)$ (read: "f of n").

Thus, $f(1) = 1^2 - 1 + 41 = 41$, $f(2) = 2^2 - 2 + 41 = 43$, $f(3) = 3^2 - 3 + 41 = 47$, etc.

If we continue to compute the values, we can generate a table:

n	$f(n)$
0	41
1	41
2	43
3	47
4	53
5	61
6	71
7	83
8	97

and so on.

Do We See Any Patterns Here?

We could continue, and indeed, you might try computing a few values, such as $f(9)$, $f(10)$, and $f(11)$. (That is, compute the expression using n = 9, 10, 11.) What strikes you about the values? For instance, did you notice that the units' digit so far is always a 1, 3, or 7? How about the numbers themselves? Is there anything special about them?

The numbers in the segment of our table are all prime numbers. We know that a prime number is a natural number greater than 1 whose *only* divisors are 1 and the number itself. The key word is the word "only" in the previous sentence.

Note how this example generates interesting questions, such as "Is the last digit in the value of the expression always 1, 3, or 7?" and "Is the expression always prime?"

Let's start with the last question of primality. How shall we proceed? Which way do we go? Do we go ahead and attempt to prove primality with a formal proof, or do we attempt to disprove the statement by producing an example in which the statement fails to hold? (We mathematicians call such an example a *counterexample*.)

Here is where things get murky. Intuition and experience with similar problems can play some role, but at this point you'll need more data to come to some conclusion.

Suppose we succeed in producing a lot more cases in which the proposition is verified. Have we proven anything definitive about the general assertion of primality? That is, have we proven the statement that our f(n) is always prime?

No! We will have shown that our f(n) produces primes for all the values tested, but nothing more. Isn't it possible that our "pattern" of getting primes breaks down at some point? Likewise, how do we know for sure that the last digits will continue to be only from among the choices 1, 3, 7?

In point of fact, one of these assertions is true, but the other is false. The statement that $n^2 - n + 41$, for n = a positive integer, is always prime, is disproven by a counterexample. Consider using n = 41. Then the expression is equal to $41 \times 41 - 41 + 41$, or the square of 41; the fact that this value is 1681 is not needed. It is enough to realize that this means that 41 is a divisor of f(41). For, this means that there is a divisor other than 1 and the value of the expression (1681).

What this illustrates is that patterns may seem to emerge where no solid pattern exists. The mathematically and scientifically minded individual therefore must take a skeptical stance toward all propositions of faith and avoid jumping to conclusions prematurely. "It is easier to destroy than to create" is the idea here: it is easier to disprove than to prove; it is easier to tear down a building than to erect one; easier to rip up a work of art than to create it in the first place.

Of course, only on the more sophisticated exams will such care be fully required. The point here is that one must not jump to conclusions based on a few examples. In practice, one may rely on "test logic" to assist in answering questions without fully considering them mathematically. Nevertheless, we are interested in problem solving in its own right here, and not just in relation to competitions.

Verifying a True Statement

Interestingly, the other statement made about the units' digit turns out to be true, a discovery I made for the first time just as I played around with this otherwise famous example. But how do we prove this? The point is that we cannot settle on examples; a counterexample might be waiting if we just try more values. No, we need some mathematical reasoning.

Just to complete the discussion, here is the essence of a proof.

The expression f(n) equals:

$$n(n+1) - 41$$

The rightmost digit in each case depends on the rightmost digit of this expression, which in turn will always be one more than that of $n(n+1)$ alone. If we look at the possible values of this, we see that there are only three values of the rightmost digit. We see this using $1 \times 2 = 2, 2 \times 3 = 6, 3 \times 4 = 12, 4 \times 5 = 20, 5 \times 6 = 30, 6 \times 7 = 42, 7 \times 8 = 56, 8 \times 9 = 72, 9 \times 10 = 90, 10 \times 11 = 110$. At this point, everything *must* repeat patternwise since we are going to use the same units' digits again. If we wished, we could fashion a more formal proof, but I hope you get the idea.

Many other general truths require more sophisticated methods to verify them, including mathematical induction, use of advanced math peculiar to the problem, and special tricks or techniques. Keep in mind, however, that most contests are not proof-oriented, so we will not make this a major focus in this book, particularly since that would be a little too ambitious for this particular book anyway.

What we've seen in this chapter is that apparent patterns may break down (as in our primality question) and fail to be real patterns, or they may persist and represent true patterns. We've seen that no number of examples can serve to prove, but just one example can disprove a general statement. Finally, to prove a conjecture (that is, an educated guess) requires some mathematical approach which does not depend on a particular value or values only.

If we understand and can work with the limitations of problem solving, not only can we discern the patterns which exist, but we can also filter out the "false alarms" which break down and do not persist.

Problems and Challenges

1. The sum of three consecutive natural numbers is always divisible by (A) 3 only (B) 5 only (C) 3 and 5 (D) 7 only (E) none of these. Note that choice (E) in this example requires more than just trial-and-error experimentation in which you look for a pattern. Can you add a proof, if needed, to handle this?

2. We earlier looked at such questions as the sum of the first 100 natural numbers. Can we develop a mathematical approach which does not depend just on the pattern of looking at some small numbers and conjecturing a formula? In other words, can you use some cleverness to add the first 100 natural numbers (1,2,3, . . .,100) other than our previous guessing of a formula for adding the first n odd numbers?

3. Likewise, by playing with patterns, you should have found earlier that a polygon of n sides has $n-3$ diagonals emanating from any one vertex. Thus, a chiliagon (a 1000-gon) has 997 diagonals at a given vertex. Can you prove this directly without recourse to arguments about patterns?

9

EXPLOITING TEST LOGIC

In an earlier exercise, I gave the question of finding the average of all the numbers involved when six of the numbers had an average of 8 and the other eight numbers had an average of 6. Suppose that this were instead a multiple-choice question. How might this enable us to find the average of the fourteen numbers more easily?

Specifically, consider choices: (A) 6 (B) 6 6/7 (C) 7 (D) 7 1/7 (E) 8.

Can you see a quick way to get the answer without really doing the formal computation? Let's reason as follows. The answer can't be 6 or 8, because if you mix numbers with an average of 6 with numbers averaging 8, the result has an average which is between these extremes. Okay, now what?

We next argue that more of the numbers have an average of 6 than 8. Therefore, the average can't be 7, as that would require an equal number of numbers averaging 6 and averaging 8. By the same token, since there are more of the smaller numbers, the average must get pulled below this 7 level. Hence, without doing any real calculations we get the answer of (B) 6 6/7, which is in fact the correct answer.

Of course, most of us understand that elimination of choices makes multiple-choice questions easier than their analogous questions without choices.

Form of Answers as Clue

Another device that we may use is our expectation that an answer has to have a certain form. Here's one from a "do-it-yourself" IQ test, that is, one of those tests designed to be like an "intelligence test" that you administer yourself and afterward score yourself.

Suppose that you have two empty pails and you need to fetch 97 pails of water from a well. How many trips to the well will this require? The choices are (A) 48 (B) 48.5 (C) 49 (D) 49.5 (E) none of these.

Most people realize quickly enough that you need to divide 97 by 2. But is the correct answer really 48.5?

A moment's thought shows that this makes no sense! How can there be a half trip? So, we have to be careful not to get seduced into thinking narrowly along these lines.

So, the answer is either 48 or 49. However, 48 trips allow for only 96 pails. Therefore, 49 is the correct answer.

We see that knowing that the answer has to be an integer (whole number) forces us to dismiss certain choices. Had we been really alert, we might have eliminated them right away. In a subsequent chapter on control, we'll look at some devices you should use to make yourself more conscious of the need not to fall for such distractors (incorrect answers).

Frequently Encountered Situations or Numbers

Some problems in geometry, most notably with right triangles, and the Pythagorean theorem in particular, fall into a related category. These are of interest in their own right as well, although many of these tend to be repeated frequently.

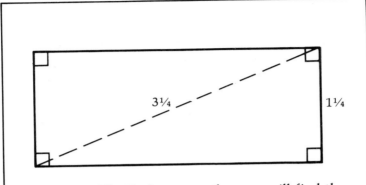

Figure 11. The Pythagorean theorem will find the missing side, but there's a shortcut here.

An old GRE general test question asked for the area of a rectangle with a diagonal of 3 1/4 and a width of 1 1/4. See Figure 11.

Let's reason as follows: The area of the rectangle may be found from the length times the width. We already know the width (given), but we don't have the length yet. So, the question now is, Can we get the length? If we look closer, we notice that there are right triangles in the rectangle, so we can use the Pythagorean theorem (the square of the hypotenuse in a right triangle equals the sum of the squares of the legs).

But here is where test logic comes into play in an otherwise routine problem. Note the fourths involved in the lengths given: 5/4 for the width and 13/4. Could this be just a familiar triangle scaled down?

Recall that most right triangles having two sides of integral length will not have the third side of integral length. Thus, a right triangle with legs of lengths 1 and 2 will have a hypotenuse with length equal to the square root of 5, which is about 2.236, and certainly not an integer. Because of this, those right triangles with lengths which are all integral have a popularity on exams greater than warranted otherwise. Thus, the 3,4,5, the 5,12,13, and the 8,15,17 triangles appear disproportionately often.

So, to return to our original question of the rectangle's area, you will see that if the diagonal is 13/4 (3 1/4) and the width is 5/4 (1 1/4), the corresponding third side must be 12/4, or 3.

In passing, let's stop to note a few interesting features of this last solution. In seeing the diagonal of the rectangle as the hypotenuse of a right triangle, we have the lesson of learning to see line segments and other figures as having several roles. (In this case, a side of a rectangle is also a side of a right triangle.) This is essential in some problems whereby that is the connection between given information and something desired.

It also reinforces an earlier theme of building a bridge between what is given and what is to be found, computed, or proven. In this case, the bridge was built backward, starting from the question (area of rectangle found how?) to seeing the need for the length, to connecting via the diagonal/hypotenuse, to getting the length and then completing the solution.

It was only at that point that our insight into getting the length quickly came into play, but once it did, the time saved was significant.

Problems and Challenges

1. Find the length of the rectangle in question directly via the Pythagorean theorem, instead of by the shortcut. Do you get 3 again? Doesn't it take a lot longer, assuming that you do get it and don't make mistakes?

2. Here's a variant of such questions. A motorist gets in her car and heads due west 70 kilometers, then heads

due north 60 kilometers, and then due west another 10 kilometers. How far is she from her original point of departure? (Note: This is *not* the same as asking how far she drove!)

3. The average of seven numbers is 9, and of another nine numbers is 7. The average of all sixteen numbers is (A) 7 1/2 (B) 7 7/8 (C) 8 1/8 (E) 8 1/2. Can this be handled as completely by a shortcut?

10 DEVELOPING CONTROL

Watch an experienced mathematician, and you will discover something remarkable.

He or she will make mistakes but will almost always seem to catch them without help from anybody else. How does the mathematician do it?

In case the significance hasn't struck you yet, control is something that you too can develop. You can learn to check yourself in ways which can minimize the probability of errors, whether they be errors of calculation or errors of analysis and theory. Armed with such a sense of control, you can solve more problems and harder problems, providing, of course, that you have a decent general knowledge of the subject matter.

Mind you, you won't develop control overnight, for it takes years of experience, education, and training. But you can begin to work on this area now, and some of the ideas apply to many of the math contests and mathematics problems you may encounter in the near future.

Is the Answer
Numerically Reasonable?

Since you may have gotten very used to using a calculator, you may be a bit rusty on some arithmetical skills.

How can you check answers, even if this is your situation?

One way is to get in the habit of estimating. Suppose that you are asked to tell which of the following numbers is larger (if either): 19.75% of 79.4, or 79.4% of 19.75.

Think about this for a moment. Then stop and answer the question.

Did you discover that there is big difference, or did you discover the quantities to be equal? Surely you noticed that the numbers used in the two parts (19.75, 79.4) were the same in both parts, but switched around in a sense. This might persuade you that the answers do in fact come out to be the same. In fact, you might enjoy knowing that a% of b is *always* equal to b% of a. That's because the first expression means $(a/100) \times b$, which equals $ab/100$, while the second similarly has the value $ba/100$. Since $ab = ba$ (commutativity of multiplication), the two are the same.

All this is fine, but suppose that you did not see any of this. Suppose you made an arithmetical error and thought you had one larger than the other. Is there no way to check other than recalculating?

Estimate by replacing 19.75 with 20, and 79.4 with 80, so that 19.75% of 79.4 is approximately 20% of 80 $= 1/5 \times 80$, or 80/5, which $= 16$. In a similar way, you should obtain 16 for the other choice. If you thought that your answers showed both expressions equal, you now feel more confident. If you thought that the two expressions were not equal (and with a significant difference), your estimate shows that the answers are, at the very least, about equal, so something is wrong. Your sense of control now tells you that you have an inconsistency, and you need to resolve it. You may not know which part is wrong, but at least you won't just go on thinking that all is well.

Spotting Contradictions

Another mechanism for control involves "estimating the situation" rather than estimating numbers.

Suppose that you saw a question such as this: Village A has a population of 2000, which declines by 100 per year, while village B has a population of 3500, which rises by 25 per year. When are the populations equal?

Careful thought shows that the populations will never be equal under these assumptions, since they are presently unequal, with the gap between them widening, not lessening.

Nevertheless, if you attempted to solve the problem, you would still have a second chance to use control to catch the difficulty. Using the approach outlined in the chapter on building bridges and working backward, we would let t = the number of years required for the desired equalization to take place. This would lead to the equation:

$$2000 - 100t = 3500 + 25t$$

Solving would yield the answer t = -12.

How should this be understood?

If you're in control, it should be a signal that something is wrong. How can the answer be negative?

The negative answer indicates that, if the hypotheses about rates of increase and decrease in the populations prevailed earlier, then 12 years *earlier*, the populations were equal.

In practice, one would not encounter such an error or question often. However, for those interested in teaching as well as problem posing, this is an important skill. Even if you're not involved with either of these, and not planning to get involved, you still need the control skill for cases where just an error in solving on your part causes the problem. In such cases, you should realize that an answer can't be negative, or of such a large or such a small size, etc.

Another Variation of the Population Question

Of course, there could be a question like the one above without the defect. Suppose the question had been worded this way: In the year 2000, village A is found to have a population of 2000, which is falling at the rate of 100 per year, with B's being 3500 and rising at the rate of 25 per year. Suppose it is also known that this has been the case for half a century. In which years are or were the populations the same or will they be the same?

As our solution above showed, the time period is -12 years, so the populations will coincide in 1988 $(2000 - 12)$.

Use Formulas Only Where Appropriate

A more flagrant error occurs if one uses a formula where it is not applicable. In such cases, the fallacy may or may not show up. In the advanced math of integral calculus, for instance, there are famous examples of what are known as "improper integrals" which fail to have a value, yet using the "usual approach" may yield a reasonable-looking result. In other areas, such as the sum of an infinite geometric series, improper use of a standard formula where not applicable may yield an answer which is clearly unbelievable. (See Exercise 3 below.) Be alert for such violations of common sense, and don't accept them uncritically.

Does the Answer
Make Sense?

In terms of error-checking, we concern ourselves with getting in the habit of asking whether the answer makes sense. Recall the problem in which you had to fetch 97 pails of water 2 at a time, and you want to know how many trips this will take (choices included 48, 48.5, and 49). Developing control would mean thinking about what an appropriate answer has to be. Once you realize it must be a whole number, you know that nonintegral values such as 48.5 are clever distractors. Once you see that, you'll probably realize you need 49 trips, not 48.

Vary the Picture
or Numbers

Another control mechanism utilizes special and extreme cases.

Suppose that you could not recall for sure whether the diagonals of a parallelogram bisect each other. Perhaps you couldn't recall either whether they are of the same length. Perhaps you recall only the definition: A parallelogram is a quadrilateral whose opposite sides are parallel.

Bearing in mind that examples can serve only to disprove, not to prove, we might try to picture a rectangle, because a rectangle is a special case of a parallelogram; specifically, a rectangle is a parallelogram with right angles. The answer is yes in this case: In a rectangle, diagonals do bisect each other and are of the same length.

But we must also consider extreme cases. What if we draw a parallelogram differently so as not to have a rectangle? As we saw in the chapter on implicit assumptions, such extremes can help us control our tendency to unconsciously accept matters based on a given diagram. See Figure 12.

Thus, an extreme diagram can serve as a clear counterexample to the notion that the diagonals are necessarily of the same length. If you draw any parallelogram, however, it should still appear that the diagonals do bisect each other.

In fact, we can prove that the diagonals do bisect each other (a standard geometry argument involving corresponding parts of congruent triangles). While we have not proven this by the diagram, at that point we may recall that such is the case, or just persuade ourselves subjectively that it is probably true. After all, during a math competition, you would not really have the time to spare for seeking a proof anyway.

Know Your Subject

The ultimate form of control, of course, is knowledge of the subject matter at a more expert level. This will help you avoid errors such as incorrect order of operations, improper cancellation with fractions, and fallacies of logic and algebra.

As a suggestion for understanding this error analysis, think of each theorem (sometimes called a rule or law) as stating: "When such and such is the situation, you may do so and so." For instance, "If a product equals zero, then at least one of the factors must equal zero, too." Note the conditions call for (1) a product and (2) the product's equaling zero. Take a simple contrast:

    A. Solve $(x - 1)(x - 2) = 0$.
    B. Solve $(x - 1) + (x - 2) = 0$.
    C. Solve $(x - 1)(x - 2) = 2$.

For A, you have a product equal to 0, so at least one factor must be 0. Therefore, set $x - 1 = 0$ and $x - 2 = 0$ separately to obtain $x = 1$ or 2.

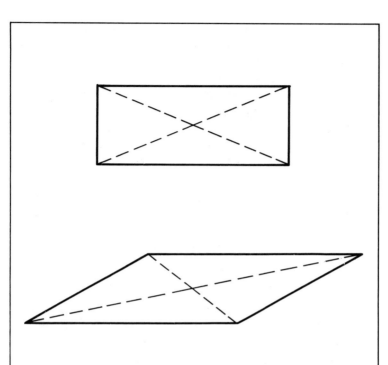

Figure 12. A special case (rectangle) and an extreme case of parallelograms. In both cases, the diagonals bisect each other, offering greater evidence for the general truth that the diagonals of a parallelogram always bisect each other. Although the diagonals have the same length in the rectangle, they don't in the other parallelogram, serving as a counter-example — and therefore a disproof — of the belief that the diagonals always have the same length.

For B, although the form is similar superficially, there is a big difference in that there is no product here. In fact, this is just a linear equation (or first-degree equation). Solving gives $2x = 3$, so $x = 3/2$, or 1.5.

For C, although we have a product again, the right side of the equation is not 0. Since it is *not* true that if a product equals 2, then one of the factors $(x - 1)$ or $(x - 2)$ must be 2, we cannot proceed as we did in A.

Instead, we would try to get the situation for this quadratic equation (or second-degree equation) to be like that of A. Expand the left side and then subtract 2 from both sides to get $x^2 - 3x = 0$. Then factor to get $x(x - 3) = 0$, so $x = 0$ or 3 (don't forget the solution from the first factor, x, being set equal to 0!).

Summary

There are many aspects to control, only some of which we've touched on here. The key point is to get in the routine of checking yourself: Are you dealing with an appropriate technique for this category of question (assuming the question falls into some neat category you can identify)? Are your numbers reasonable? Is the sign reasonable? Should the answer be a whole number?

Developing a skeptical attitude—trying to find errors rather than hoping you're right without really critically examining matters—is important in this process, whether using special cases, extreme cases, estimation, or other approaches.

Do these things, and you'll start catching your errors the way mathematicians do.

Problems and Challenges

Without adding, calculating, or solving, tell why these situations are actually contradictory:

1. Adding up $1 + 2 + 3 + \ldots + 100$ using the formula $1 + 2 + 3 + \ldots + n = n(n + 1)/2$, to get 50. (Note: don't use the formula for the check!)

2. Adding $1 + 2 + 3 + \ldots + 100$ using the same formula, to get 500.5 as the answer. (Again, don't use the formula.)

3. Summing the infinite geometric series $1 + 2 + 4 + 8 + \ldots$, with ratio $r = 2$ and leading term $a = 1$, using the known formula

$$\text{Sum} = a/(1 - r) = 1/(1-2) = -1$$

4. What is wrong with the following situation? Triangle ABC is similar to DEF, with the latter having sides of lengths DE $= 5.5$, DF $= 5.5$, and EF $= 14$. AB corresponds to DE, AC to DF, and AB $= 4$. (Remember that corresponding sides are proportional and corresponding angles have the same measure for similar triangles.) You are asked for the perimeter of triangle ABC. (Hint: Try to draw triangle DEF first.)

11

CHANGING FORMS; MISCELLANEOUS MATTERS

Look at all the paths available for a city dweller to go from point A to point B, as in Figure 13. How many such paths are there?

ERROR   SOME PATHS MISSING FROM DISCUSSION

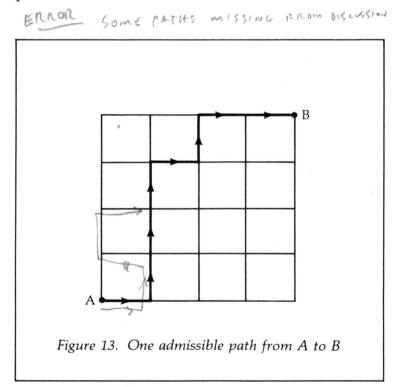

Figure 13. One admissible path from A to B

For purposes of this question, we assume that the pedestrian will take only one of the direct routes which proceed one block at a time, in each case choosing east or north. (It would be pointless to ever walk in a direction which does not help get from A to B.)

If we attempt a direct, "brute force" approach, we will undoubtedly fail, as the number of possibilities is too large. We instead need to reinterpret the question.

Our problem is that we need to do the counting, but we cannot do it by the actual listing of possibilities and then counting. We saw earlier that we could do this with various counting principles. The study of such is combinatorics, sometimes considered to be "the mathematics of counting without really counting" (in the conventional sense). That is what is called for here. However, there is another ingredient as well.

Change the Form

Looking at the question again, we may note that any path from A to B amounts to a choice of R's (for right) and U's (for up). For example, the path in which you go right, right, up, right, up, up, up, right may be viewed as the sequence (R,R,U,R,U,U,U,R). What would be the sequence of R's and U's for the path in Figure 13? Write it down before reading further.

If you saw the path in the figure as (R,U,U,U,R,U, R,R), then you're on the right path! Notice that each such path has a corresponding sequence, and vice versa. Moreover, different such paths have different corresponding sequences, and different such sequences have different corresponding paths.

Aha! The question is now one of *counting how many such sequences there are*. Note that there must be four R's and four U's in each sequence, or else the resulting path will not end at B. What does this in turn mean to us?

It means that we are asking how many ways there

are of picking four spots of eight to be designated R, and the other four spots therefore to be designated U. You must realize, however, that once you identify the four to be picked as U, you have no choice left for the location of the spots to be R.

So, the question is mathematically equivalent to the reduced, more standard one of counting the number of ways to choose four locations from eight; that is, to choose four items out of eight.

For this, we review a few standard results from eleventh-grade mathematics. First, recall that the number of ways to choose four things from eight is sometimes denoted 8 C 4 (there are other notations). Second, recall the factorial notation: n! (read: "n factorial") is n times $(n-1)$ times $(n-2)$ . . . times 3 times 2 times 1. For instance, $4! = 4 \times 3 \times 2 \times 1 = 24$.

The first two points are only definitions, but the third point is a mathematical formula. (If you haven't had it yet, it may be in a future course or later in your present course. For now, take it on faith or ask a teacher.) That result gives us 8 C 4 = $8!/(4!4!)$. Even if this is new, you should be able to calculate 8 C 4. Note the many "cancellations" to get down to $(8 \times 7 \times 6 \times 5)/(4 \times 3 \times 2 \times 1)$, which then gives 70.

Hence, there are exactly seventy distinct paths from A to B in the figure.

One of the features of the above situation is the strategic "shifting of gears" when confronted with difficulty. We converted from one form to another. We took a given question about paths and converted it to a question about sequences. Next, we reinterpreted the question to be one involving combinations. Lastly, we counted the number of such sequences using a standard result about combinations. Changing forms and changing variables are important strategies in mathematical problem solving.

Although this example would have to be classified

as difficult, particularly if you've never seen anything like it before, the alternative of having to draw all paths is far, far worse. It would actually take an extremely long time, you'd probably make numerous errors, the listing is bound to be unpleasant, and there is a total lack of elegance in the listing approach.

Reductionism

Consider this more algebraic question as another illustration of the value of changing forms. I call the process of switching to a simpler form "reductionism." Let's see how this works in another difficult problem.

Let $x > 0$. What is the smallest possible value of the following expression? What about the largest?: $160x^2 + 320 + 160/x^2$.

This problem is formidable for most students. First, let's try to make some sense of it. If we use values such as $x = 1, 2, 3, 4, 5$, and so on, we see that the values of the expression seem to grow. In view of the form of the expression, it should be clear that there is no maximum value, for we can let x be as large as we please.

The more interesting and appropriate question is to find the minimum value—assuming one exists! We cannot merely accept this, as we have just seen with the question of a maximum. How do we know that using smaller and smaller fractional values of x, for instance, won't produce smaller and smaller values for the expression? We obviously cannot try every value, as there are infinitely many. We need something analytical to resolve the matter.

Let's see how we can attack this by an appropriate simplification. Rewrite the expression by factoring. First, common factor out the 160, and then note that the other factor is really the square of a binomial. Hence, you should get: $160(x + 1/x)^2$.

That is the first part of the reductionism. The second

is to note what this now requires. For instance, we can ignore the role of the 160, for the smaller the other factor, $(x + 1/x)^2$, is, the smaller 160 times it will be. But $(x + 1/x)^2$ is smallest when $(x + 1/x)$ is smallest.

Thus, the question boils down to dealing with the simpler matter of the minimum of $x + 1/x$ for $x > 0$. While even this is not trivial if you've never been exposed to it before, it is certainly a lot easier. And, if you have dealt with this before, then you see how we've *reduced* the question to a simpler one. Reductionism—changing form or content so as to make the solution of a harder problem boil down to a simpler one—is a useful approach for problem solvers. Keep it in mind, along with the general matter of changing forms, for it can be a wonderful "weapon" in your "arsenal" for "executing" tricky maneuvers.

Let's finish this example, now. We can experiment using values such as $x = 1$, $x = 1/2$, or $x = 1/3$ to persuade ourselves, at least tentatively, that the least value of $x + 1/x$, for $x > 0$, is 2, achieved by using $x = 1$. On a nonessay exam (e.g., multiple choice), we could satisfy ourselves by having tried different kinds of numbers: integers and fractions. Combined with our earlier argument, we would be satisfied of the correctness, at least subjectively.

While this does not provide a complete proof, it is adequate in this case. There are several ways to prove the result about $x + 1/x$ using inequalities or calculus, but we won't take them up here.

Still, we know now to use $x = 1$ to get the answer, so the minimum is then just $160(1 + 1/1)^2$, which equals 640, the answer.

Another Important Change

Sometimes a change of variable does the trick. For instance, suppose that you had to solve the equation:

$$x^6 - 9x^3 + 8 = 0.$$

You've never solved a sixth-degree equation, perhaps? Take another look and notice that there are only three terms (of a possible seven for a sixth-degree polynomial), and these are of degrees 6, 3, and 0. Based on these being in arithmetic sequence, this suggests a change of variable.

Let $u = x^3$, so we get
$u^2 - 9u + 8 = 0$.
Factor: $(u - 1)(u - 8) = 0$.
Hence, $u - 1 = 0$ or $u - 8 = 0$.
Thus, $u = 1$ or $u = 8$.
But now $u = x^3$, so $x^3 = 1$ or 8.
Hence, $x = 1$ or 2.

Changing forms and changing variables, as well as reducing to simpler forms, are among the most useful tools for handling problems which sometimes only seem insoluble.

Problems and Challenges

1. In the same diagram (Figure 13), which of the seventy admissible paths from A to B is longest? Shortest? Explain your answer.

2. What is the largest possible value of the expression $10x^2 - 20x^4$? (Hint: The expression is quadratic in form.) Is there a minimum?

3. This question comes from the first annual AIME examination (1983): Let $f(x) = |x - p| + |x - 15| + |x - p - 15|$, where $0 < p < 15$. Determine the minimum value taken by $f(x)$ for x in the interval $p \leq x \leq 15$. (As usual, $|x| =$ the absolute value of x.)

4. Also from the 1983 AIME: What is the product of the real roots of the equation $x^2 + 18x + 30 = 2\sqrt{x^2-18x+45}$?

5. If you walk from one vertex of a square, X, to a diagonally opposite vertex, Y, about what percent less distance is that to walk than if you walk along the sides to go from X to Y?

12

No book of this small size can cover the almost infinite variety of questions and topics encountered in problem solving for competitions.

In particular, I have had to compromise and omit topics, even though I know that they occur. Thus, there has been little here in the way of inequalities, trigonometry, logarithms, and coordinate systems, to name some.

For extra practice, here are some more questions and four sample exams of widely varying difficulty. The exams are the AJHSME (for junior high school), the Gauss (which is given to junior high school students in Canada), the AHSME (for high school), and the AIME (for advanced students of any grade who can qualify). The AJHSME material is the entire sample examination provided with the invitation for the first actual AJHSME. The AHSME problems appeared in a recent AHSME information booklet and were taken from several previous AHSME exams. You can work on these questions with a friend, a teacher, or a fellow student.

Don't be discouraged. Some questions may be beyond your ability, while others may just be hard.

Mixed-Bag Problems

1. The Cake-Cutting Problem. Given a piece of cake in the form of a rectangular solid with a square top, and

with icing on all faces except the bottom, show how to cut the cake into five pieces each having the same amount of icing and the same amount of cake. Each cut should be vertical—that is, made perpendicular to the square top. Each person must receive his or her cake all in one piece only.

2. Find the fallacy in this "proof" that $1 = 2$:
   Let $a = b$. Then $a \times a = a \times b$, so $a \times a - b \times b = a \times b - b \times b$. Now factor (difference of squares on the left, common factoring on the right) to get $(a-b)(a+b) = b(a-b)$. Dividing both sides by $a-b$ now gives $a+b = b$, but since $a = b$ from the original assumption, we have $2b = b$, or $1=2$.

3. Suppose that you are offered any salary you wish—any positive number at all—subject to the stipulation that the tax on it, as a percent, will be the same percent as the number of thousands in the salary. For instance, if you opt for $40,000 as your salary, you will have to pay 40% in taxes. How much should you choose for your gross so as to have the maximum possible net amount left after taxes? (While a computer program can help, can you handle this using, at most, precalculus?) Can you prove your answer to be correct?

4. The McDonald's Permuted Change (a true story). In late 1976, I went to McDonald's and spent $1.85 for a quarter-pounder, large fries, and a Coke. I gave the clerk $10.00, and my change was $8.15! Note that the digits of the price and the change are the same. Find all other prices with this property that the change from $10.00 produces change with the same digits (occurring in the same frequency).

5. Using a small postcard and a scissors, can you pass your body through the postcard?

6. The Army Problem. What is the smallest-size army which can be lined up into rows and columns in exactly sixty-four ways? (This one is not that easy.)

7. Hooks, wrenches, screwdrivers. Suppose that these cost, respectively, $0.50, $10, and $3 each. You buy 100 tools total from these, and you spend exactly $100. How many of each do you buy? (Caution: does this implicitly suggest a unique solution? Would such an assumption be justified?)

8. (A) What is the smallest number which, when divided by 2, leaves a remainder of 1, and, when divided by 3, leaves a remainder of 2? (B) What if it also had to leave a remainder of 3 when divided by 4?

9. Milk and coffee. Pour equal quantities of milk and coffee separately into two identical cups. Now take a spoonful of coffee and pour into the milk. Stir. Now take a spoonful of the milk (diluted by a bit of coffee) and pour into the coffee. Question: Is there more milk in the coffee, or more coffee in the milk?

10. Can an irrational number to an irrational power produce a rational answer? What about a rational number to a rational power producing an irrational answer? What are the other six analogous questions? And the answers?

11. Angles and clocks. Intermediate question: What angle do the hands of a clock make at 3:15?

12. More angles and clocks. Hard question: At exactly what time a few minutes before 2:00 do the hands of a clock produce a right angle?

13. Waker-upper. Take 14 from 31; what do you have?

14. Find two whole numbers whose product is one million and yet such that neither has zero in the number's decimal representation.

15. Each time a hobo finds five cigar butts, he can produce a cigar. One day, he finds twenty-five butts. How many cigars can he smoke?

16. Given a square piece of paper, tell how, using only folds to produce creases, you can form or determine angles with tangents of 1, 2, and 3 in as few creases as possible. Can you do it with just four creases? How about three? (Note: You need a crease just to locate a midpoint of a side.)

AJHSME SAMPLE EXAMINATION

1.

$12 - 11 + 10 - 9 + 8 - 7 + 6 - 5 + 4 - 3 + 2 - 1 =$

A) -12   B) -6   C) 0   D) 6   E) 12

2. According to the circle graph (which is drawn to scale), about what percent of tax money is spent on education?

A) 10%   B) 20%   C) 30%   D) 50%   E) 70%

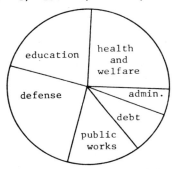

Where Do Your Taxes Go?

3. $\frac{3}{5} \div \frac{5}{6}$ written as a decimal is

A) .5   B) 1.3888...   C) .72
D) 1.4333...   E) 2.0

4. The difference between the largest number and the smallest number in the set {.5, .505, .55, .5005} is

A) .005   B) .045   C) .0495   D) .05   E) .055

5. The best estimate of the area of rectangle ABCD, in square units, is

A) .8   B) 1.2   C) 4.8   D) 6   E) 8

6. The product 737 x 767 is closest to which of the following:

A) 50,000   B) 55,000   C) 60,000   D) 500,000
E) 550,000

7. Using a calculator, a student mistakenly multiplied by 10 when he should have divided by 10. The incorrect answer displayed was 600. The correct answer is

A) .6   B) 6   C) 60   D) 6000   E) 60,000

8. PQ is a straight line. The number of degrees in angle VTS is

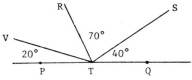

   A) 80   B) 90   C) 100   D) 110   E) 120

9. Compute:

$$\frac{597+598+599+600+601+602+603+604+605+606}{5}$$

   A) 1201   B) 1203   C) 1205   D) 1206   E) 1208

10. $\sqrt{49} - \sqrt{9} =$

   A) 2   B) 4   C) $\sqrt{7} - \sqrt{3}$ D) $\sqrt{40}$ E) 10

11. 0.5% of 246 is

   A) .123   B) 1.23   C) 12.3   D) 123   E) 1230

12. An airplane flies 1000 miles due west in 3 hours and then flies 1000 miles due east in 2 hours. The average speed of the airplane for the entire 2000 mile trip is

   A) 200 mph   B) $208\frac{1}{3}$ mph   C) $333\frac{1}{3}$ mph

   D) 400 mph   E) $416\frac{2}{3}$ mph

13. A girl had her monthly allowance doubled, received an additional $3 increase, and then had her allowance cut in half. How much is her present allowance compared to her original allowance?

   A) $1.50 less   B) the same   C) $1.50 more

   D) $3 more   E) $4.50 more

14. The sum of the smallest odd prime, the largest prime less than 50, and the smallest prime greater than 60 is

   A) 110   B) 111   C) 113   D) 115   E) 117

15. After being discounted 20%, a coat sells for $30.00. The original selling price of the coat was

   A) $24   B) $32   C) $36   D) $37.50   E) $42.50

16. IF 3! = 3x2x1 = 6, 4! = 4x3x2x1 = 24 and so
on, then $\dfrac{8!}{6!}$ =

 A) $\dfrac{4}{3}$ B) 4 C) 8 D) 28 E) 56

17. Identical cubes are
stacked in the corner
of a room as shown.
How many of the cubes
are not visible?

 A) 10   B) 12

 C) 15   D) 18

 E) 20

18. What is the area, in
square units, of the
triangular region if
the shaded area is
1 square unit?

 A) 2   B) 2.25

 C) 2.5   D) 3

 E) 3.5

19. If there are exactly four Sundays in October,
then October 31 could <u>not</u> fall on a

 A) Tuesday B) Wednesday C) Thursday

 D) Friday   E) Saturday

20. A party is scheduled for an open area of the
park and a tent has been ordered. There is a
50% chance of rain. Whether it rains or not,
there is a 50% chance that the tent will not
arrive in time for the party. Of the following
which best describes the chance that the
partygoers get wet (assuming they will not get
wet if the tent arrives in time)?

 A) certain to be wet
 B) 3 chances in 4 to be wet
 C) chances even to be wet or dry
 D) 1 chance in 4 to be wet
 E) certain to be dry

21. An "hourglass" consists of two identical cones contained in the right cylinder of radius 2.5 cm and height 6 cm. The top cone is filled with sand. The volume of a cylinder equals the product of the area of its base and its height. The volume of a cone equals one-third of the product of the area of its base and its height. The ratio of the volume of sand to the volume of the cylinder is

A) $\frac{1}{8}$ B) $\frac{1}{6}$ C) $\frac{1}{4}$ D) $\frac{1}{3}$ E) $\frac{1}{2}$

22. A crowd watching a parade fills the sidewalks of Fifth Avenue for a distance of 2 miles on each side. The sidewalks are 10 feet wide and an average person requires 4 square feet to stand on. A good estimate of the size of the crowd is

A) 25,000 people   B) 50,000 people
C) 100,000 people D) 250,000 people
E) 500,000 people

23. The average price of hamburger goes up 10% the first month, goes down 10% the second month, and goes up 10% the third month. By what percent did the average price of hamburger go up from its initial price to its price at the end of the third month?

A) 10% B) 9.9% C) 9.5% D) 8.9% E) 8.5%

24. Let r be a real number, positive, negative, or zero. Which of the following numbers is always greater than r ?

A) $r^2 + 1$ B) $2r$ C) $\sqrt{r^2 + r}$
D) $(r + 1)^3$ E) r^{100}

25. Sam and Dave run a 50 m race, Sam winning by 10 m. (When Sam crosses the finish line, Dave is exactly 10 m behind). The run a second 50 m race with Same starting 10 m behind the original starting line. What is the outcome of the second race if each runs at the same constant speed he did in the first race?

A) Dave wins by 1 m   B) They tie
C) Sam wins by 1 m   D) Sam wins by 2 m
E) Sam wins by 2.5 m

ANSWERS AND SELECTED SOLUTIONS TO SAMPLE QUESTIONS

1. D   2. B   3. C   4. D   5. A   6. E   7. B

8. E   9. B   10. B   11. B   12. D   13. C   14. B

15. D   16. E   17. E   18. C   19. A   20. D   21. B

22. B   23. D   24. A   25. D

9. (B) The addends can be grouped in pairs

$$597 + 606 = 1203$$
$$598 + 605 = 1203$$
$$599 + 604 = 1203$$
$$600 + 603 = 1203$$
$$601 + 602 = 1203$$

Hence the desired number equals $\frac{5(1203)}{5} = 1203$.

17. (E) There are 4 hidden cubes below the single cube in the top layer (4); there are 3 hidden cubes under each of the 2 cubes showing in the second layer from the top (2x3 = 6); there are 2 hidden cubes under each of the 3 cubes showing in the third layer (3x2 = 6); and 1 cube under each of the 4 cubes showing in the fourth layer (4x1 = 4) for a total of 20 cubes.

18. (C) Consider the 2 x 3 rectangular region enclosing the triangle. Subtract from this area the areas of the three unwanted triangles. Thus the area of the triangle is

$$6 - \frac{1}{2}(1)(2) - \frac{1}{2}(1)(3) - \frac{1}{2}(2)(1) = 2.5.$$

19. (A) Since there are exactly four Sundays in the month, the last Sunday cannot fall on the 29th, 30th or 31st. Therefore the 31st cannot fall on a Tuesday. For example, if the last Sunday were on the 29th, then there would be four other Sundays - the 1st, 8th, 15th and 22nd - and the 31st would be on a Tuesday.

23. (D) If P is the initial price of hamburger, then the price after the changes is

$$\underbrace{(1.1)}_{\substack{10\% \\ \text{inc.}}} \underbrace{(.9)}_{\substack{10\% \\ \text{dec.}}} \underbrace{(1.1)}_{\substack{10\% \\ \text{inc.}}} P = 1.089P,$$

so there is 8.9% increase

or

If the initial price is thought of as 100%, then a 10% increase gives 110%. A 10% decrease give 110-11 = 99% and a second 10% increase give 99 + 9.9 = 108.9% for an increase of 8.9%.

25. (D) Dave runs 40 m in the same time Sam runs 50 m, so the ratio of their rates is 4 to 5. For the 60 m Sam runs in the second race, Dave will run $\frac{4}{5}$ x 60 m = 48 m. Thus Sam wins by 2 m.

SAMPLE GAUSS DIVISION PROBLEMS

[The paper, designed for grade 7 and 8 students, consists of 26 multiple-choice problems.]

1. If $\dfrac{N}{72} = \dfrac{5}{18}$, N equals

    (A) 20   (B) 16   (C) 15   (D) 14   (E) 12

2. The perimeter of the given figure is

    (A) 36 cm   (B) 44 cm   (C) 52 cm

    (D) 60 cm   (E) 72 cm

    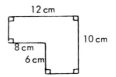

3. Five boys wrote a mathematics test. The average mark was 68. If the marks of four boys were 75, 62, 84 and 53, the mark of the fifth boy was

    (A) 66   (B) 68   (C) 76   (D) 68.5   (E) 56

4. A student using an electronic calculator mistakenly multiplies by 10 instead of dividing by 10. The incorrect answer on display is 600. The correct answer is

    (A) 0.6   (B) 6   (C) 60   (D) 6 000   (E) 60 000

5. John has 400 spaghetti strands, each 15 cm long, on his lunch plate. If he joined them end to end using sauce as glue) to form one long strand, the length of his lunch would be

    (A) 6 km   (B) 60 m   (C) 600 cm   (D) 6 000 mm   (E) 60 000 cm

6. Sir Lance needs a lot of ladder to reach the top of a castle wall. At the base of the wall is a moat 5 metres wide filled with crocodiles. His 13 metre ladder just reaches the top of the wall from the edge of the moat. The height of the wall, in metres, is

    (A) $\sqrt{8}$ (B) 12   (C) 8   (D) $\sqrt{18}$ (E) $\sqrt{194}$

7. Rearranging the digits of the number 579 produces different numbers. The sum of all such numbers, including 579, is

    (A) 4662   (B) 4065   (C) 3705   (D) 3687   (E) 3303

8. The numbers 1, 2, 3, 4, are placed in the empty squares so that each row, each column, and each diagonal contains each of the four numbers. The sum of the numbers in the two squares marked with an asterisk (*) is

1	2	3	4
4			1
*	*		

    (A) 3   (B) 4   (C) 5   (D) 6   (E) 7

Annual High School Mathematics
Examination Sample Problems

1. If $y=2x$ and $z=2y$, then $x+y+z$ equals
   (A) x (B) $3x$ (C) $5x$ (D) $7x$ (E) $9x$

2. The largest whole number such that seven times the number is less than 100 is
   (A) 12   (B) 13   (C) 14   (D) 15   (E) 16

3. In triangle ABC, $AB=AC$ and $\angle A=80°$. If points D, E and F lie on sides BC, AC and AB, respectively, and $CE=CD$ and $BF=BD$, then $\angle EDF$ equals

   (A) $30°$ (B) $40°$
   (C) $50°$ (D) $65°$
   (E) none of these

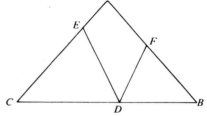

4. Find the sum of the digits of the largest even three digit number (in base ten representation) which is not changed when its unit's and hundred's digits are interchanged.
   (A) 22   (B) 23   (C) 24   (D) 25   (E) 26

5. The square of an integer is called a *perfect square*. If x is a perfect square, the next larger perfect square is
   (A) $x+1$ (B) x^2+1 (C) x^2+2x+1 (D) x^2+x
   (E) $x+2\sqrt{x}+1$

6. A man walks x miles due west, turns $150°$ to his left and walks 3 miles in the new direction. If he finishes at a point $\sqrt{3}$ miles from his starting point, then x is
   (A) $\sqrt{3}$ (B) $2\sqrt{3}$ (C) $\frac{3}{2}$ (D) 3
   (E) not uniquely determined by the given information

7. Find a positive integral solution to the equation
   $$\frac{1+3+5+\cdots+(2n-1)}{2+4+6+\cdots+2n} = \frac{115}{116}.$$
   (A) 110   (B) 115   (C) 116   (D) 231
   (E) The equation has no positive integral solutions.

8. In $\triangle ADE$. $\angle ADE = 140°$ and points B and C lies on sides AD and AE. respectively. If lengths AB. BC. CD and DE are all equal, then the measure of $\angle EAD$ is
(A) 5°   (B) 6°   (C) 7.5°   (D) 8°   (E) 10°

9. If an integer n. greater than 8, is a solution of the equation $x^2 - ax + b = 0$ and the representation of a in the base n numeration system is 18, then the base n representation of b is
(A) 18   (B) 28   (C) 80   (D) 81   (E) 280

10. A store prices an item in dollars and cents so that when 4% sales tax is added no rounding is necessary because the result is exactly n dollars where n is a positive integer. The smallest value of n is
(A) 1   (B) 13   (C) 25   (D) 26   (E) 100

11. Sides AB. BC and CD of (simple) quadrilateral $ABCD$ have lengths 4, 5 and 20, respectively. If vertex angles B and C are obtuse and $\sin C = -\cos B = \frac{3}{5}$, then side AD has length
(A) 24   (B) 24.5   (C) 24.6   (D) 24.8   (E) 25

12. The function f satisfies the functional equation
$$f(x) + f(y) = f(x+y) - xy - 1$$
for every pair x. y of real numbers. If $f(1) = 1$, then the number of integers $n \neq 1$ for which $f(n) = n$ is
(A) 0   (B) 1   (C) 2   (D) 3   (E) infinite

13. In $\triangle ABC$. $AB = 10$, $AC = 8$ and $BC = 6$. Circle P is the circle with smallest radius which passes through C and is tangent to AB. Let Q and R be the points of intersection, distinct from C. of circle P with sides AC and BC. respectively. The length of segment QR is
(A) 4.75   (B) 4.8   (C) 5
(D) $4\sqrt{2}$ (E) $3\sqrt{3}$

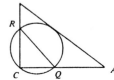

14. An ordered pair $(b. c)$ of integers, each of which has absolute value less than or equal to five, is chosen at random, with each such ordered pair having an equal likelihood of being chosen. What is the probability that the equation $x^2 + bx + c = 0$ will *not* have distinct positive real roots?

(A) $\frac{106}{121}$ (B) $\frac{108}{121}$ (C) $\frac{110}{121}$ (D) $\frac{112}{121}$
(E) none of these

Answers: 1D, 2C, 3C, 4D, 5E, 6E, 7B, 8E, 9C, 10B, 11E, 12B, 13B, 14E.

THE ANNUAL

AMERICAN INVITATIONAL MATHEMATICS EXAMINATION

(AIME)

TUESDAY, MARCH .., 19..

A Prize Examination Sponsored by:

MATHEMATICAL ASSOCIATION OF AMERICA

SOCIETY OF ACTUARIES

MU ALPHA THETA

NATIONAL COUNCIL OF TEACHERS OF MATHEMATICS

CASUALTY ACTUARIAL SOCIETY

INSTRUCTIONS

1. Do not open this booklet until told to do so.

2. This is a 15 question, 2.5 hour examination with integer answers. Your score will be the number of answers you get right. There is no partial credit.

3. All your answers, and certain other information, are to be recorded on a computer card. Your Examination Manager will instruct you how to fill out the card after you have finished with these instructions. Only the computer card and this cover sheet will be collected from you.

4. Scratch paper, graph paper, ruler, compass and eraser are permitted. Calculators and slide rules are not permitted.

5. Please print the following:

_____
Last Name   First Name   Middle Initial

_____
Home Street Address

_____
City   State or Province   Zip or Postcode

_____
Home Phone including Area Code   Your Age

_____
Full Name of School   Grade Level (e.g., 11)

6. This AIME is the qualifying examination for the U.S.A. Mathematical Olympiad (USAMO) to be given on May .., 19... Please check one box:

If I qualify for the USAMO, I agree to take it.   YES ☐   NO ☐

Your school must also agree to administer the USAMO before you can take it.

[This Sample AIME may be duplicated without further permission.]

SAMPLE AMERICAN INVITATIONAL MATHEMATICS EXAMINATION

1. The lines L and K are symmetric to each other with respect to the line $y = x$. The equation of L is $y = \frac{1}{30}x - \frac{1}{15}$ The equation of K is $y = mx + b$. Find mb.

2. Find x if $(x/9)^{\log_7 9} - (x/11)^{\log_7 11} = 0$.

3. Given that $i^2 = -1$, find the largest positive integer n for which $(n + i)^4$ is an integer.

4. Two identical jars are filled with alcohol solutions, the ratio of volume of alcohol to the volume of water being 3:1 in one jar and 4:1 in the other jar. If the entire contents of the two jars are mixed together, the ratio of the volume of alcohol to the volume of water in the mixture is r:1. If r is expressed as a fraction in lowest terms, what is the sum of the numerator and denominator?

5. If r is a number such that $8x^3 - 4x^2 - 42x + 45$ is divisible by $(x - r)^2$, then what is 10r ?

6. How many real solutions has the equation $\frac{x}{100} = \sin x$?

7. What is the smallest positive integer n such that
$$\sqrt{n} - \sqrt{n - 1} < .1 ?$$

8. In a triangle with sides of lengths a, b and c, we have

   $(a + b + c)(a + b - c) = 3ab$. Find the degree measure of the

   angle opposite the side of length c .

9. In $\triangle ABC$, AB = 5 , AC = 4 and BC = 3. Circle P is the

   circle with smallest radius which passes through C and is

   tangent to AB. Let Q and R be the points of intersection,

   distinct from C, of the circle P with sides AC and BC,

   respectively. If x is the length of segment QR, what is 100x ?

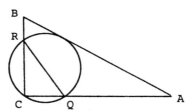

10. The largest real solution to $\sqrt{100 - \sqrt{100 + x}} = x$ can

    be written in the form $\dfrac{a + \sqrt{b}}{c}$, where a, b, c are integers

    with no common factor. What is b ?

11. Alice, Bob and Carol repeatedly take turns tossing a die. Alice

    begins; Bob always follows Alice; Carol always follows Bob; and

    Alice always follows Carol. The probability of obtaining a six

    on any one toss is 1/6, independent of the outcome of any other

    toss. Let P be the probability that Carol is the first to toss

    a six. If P is written as a fraction in lowest terms, what is

    the sum of the numerator and denominator?

12. Four balls of radius 2 are mutually tangent, three resting on the floor and the fourth resting on the others. A tetrahedron, each of whose edges has length s, is circumscribed around the balls. To the nearest integer, what is s ?

13. In a tennis tournament, n women and 2n men play, and each player plays exactly one match with every other player. There are no ties and the ratio of the number of matches won by women to the number of matches won by men is 7/5. Find n .

14. In ΔABC, the length of AC is 8, the point E is the midpoint of side BC, and D is on side AC. The degree measures of relevant angles are as labeled in the figure below. Let K be the sum of the area of ΔABC and twice the area of Δ CDE. To the nearest integer, what is K ?

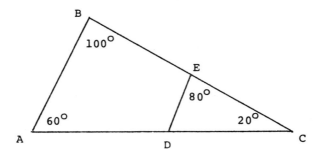

15. A six-digit number (base ten) is <u>squarish</u> if it satisfies the following conditions: (i) none of its digits is zero; (ii) it is a perfect square; and (iii) the first two digits, the middle two digits and the last two digits of the number are all perfect squares when considered as two-digit numbers. Find the leftmost three digits of the largest squarish number.

ANSWERS

The problems on this Sample Examination were adapted from the Annual High School Mathematics Examinations (AHSME) of 1978 through 1981. Changes, sometimes major, were made in the wording so as to obtain unique integer answers between 0 and 999. Actual AIME problems will of course be originals. Below are the answers for this Sample, followed by the year and problem number of the corresponding problem on the AHSME. Complete solutions to these AHSME problems may be had by ordering the appropriate AHSME Solutions Pamphlets from Prof. Walter E. Mientka, 917 Oldfather Hall, University of Nebraska, Lincoln NE 68588.

1. 60 (81, #10)	6. 63 (81, #18)	11. 116 (81, #26)
2. 99 (81, #15)	7. 26 (78, #18)	12. 14 (80, #26)
3. 1 (80, #17)	8. 60 (81, #21)	13. 3 (78, #30)
4. 31 (79, #15)	9. 240 (78, #26)	14. 14 (79, #30)
5. 15 (80, #24)	10. 397 (81, #29)	15. 646 (80, #30)

13

A FINAL WORD OF ADVICE

Engaging in a competition, even a voluntary one, makes even the best "players" nervous sometimes. It is natural. It is to be expected. It is even desirable, as it keeps you sharp and prepares you for what is to come. It is part of our evolutionary survival mechanism which gets the heart racing and the adrenaline pumping.

Here are some ideas on how to cope with this anxiety and how to improve your chances of doing well in competition.

The most obvious thing to do is to prepare well for the months or even years that you may have available before competing. Set aside time each day to help prepare. (Cramming won't work.) Are there copies of previous exams which you may work and practice on? If you are planning to become involved with a particular contest, see whether your school has a math club or math team that will give encouragement, teach extra techniques and tricks, and offer camaraderie or support for your efforts. Seeing others with the same interest reinforces your good feelings about what you are doing, and you help yourself and others by such participation.

True, some of these same students will be competitors. They may be competitors to get on a math team. Or, more likely, they may become competitors for getting the best score in your school. But, just as athletes group together and exchange ideas, giving one another moral support in the process, "mathletes" can do the same for each other.

The second important thing, after you've spent a measure of time and energy in learning and preparing, is to keep things in perspective, and be realistic. Many people advocate teaching people that their mental attitude can turn them into winners. And you do need to use any anxiety that you have and channel it into improving, into believing in yourself, and into being the best you can be. Who can argue with this sort of advice? But most of us can only go so far even if we do this.

Learning is a lifelong process. The satisfactions and skills you acquire will not disappear after that particular contest is over. And there are always other contests. You can work on improving your skills, and not just think about beating other people.

We should face the fact that most of us will not have our lives determined by how we do on a particular competition. Our futures probably do not hang in the balance. So, be reasonable and keep things in perspective. Sure, try to do well, and use your nervous energy. Work and learn. But don't engage in needless worry either before, during, or after any particular contest. It is simply not worth it.

Third, do something relaxing the day and night before the competition. Little can be gained by any kind of cramming. Relax. Go to a movie. Do you like tennis? You get the point. Unwind a little.

Make sure you get plenty of sleep that night. In fact, your general daily habits are important in your preparation, including your health habits relating to sleep, nutrition, physical as well as mental exercise, and so on.

The day of the exam, be sure to get up early enough so as to allow extra time for travel. Make sure, the night before, that you have all materials you need. Do you have extra pencils with erasers, if they are not to be provided at the contest site? Are you allowed calculators or other tools? Being on time, or better, at least a few minutes early, with all you need, makes a big difference psychologically in preparing you. Those who come late or without what they need are not aware that they subconsciously are losing out on more than just precious minutes. Their disorientation puts them at a disadvantage. Don't put yourself at a disadvantage.

As further preparation, make sure you are familiar with the scoring formula to be employed. Does it hurt to guess? If so, how many choices should you have to eliminate before it becomes advantageous to guess? Your strategy should be mapped out long before you enter the test area!

You must also be prepared to deal with the format of the exam. Are the questions to be answered via a multiple-choice format? Do you have to pencil in little boxes for computer scoring? Are there special directions? If you don't know what the format is, it is best to ask a teacher or somebody connected to the contest to provide the information, as you may do much better being prepared for special formats. You will find that this will be good advice for other kinds of exams you may encounter, particularly those offered by the Educational Testing Service and used for application to college or graduate school.

Do your best. Keep in mind the techniques you've learned. But remember, again, not to take things so seriously that you let your future happiness hinge on how well or poorly you do. Just participating is a sign of courage and confidence, and you can afford to feel pretty good about yourself, no matter how you do! Few people accomplish even that much! Congratulations to you!

SOLUTIONS TO PROBLEMS AND CHALLENGES

Chapter 1

1. SIX

2. One solution is provided in Figure 14. But how does one logically arrive at such a solution, without resort to a lot of experimentation?

Each of the two middlemost little squares touches all the others (horizontally, vertically, or diagonally) *except one*. For instance, the box with the 1 in it in the solution, touches the boxes bearing the numbers (clockwise from top) 3, 5, 8, 6, 4, 7. The only box it doesn't touch is the

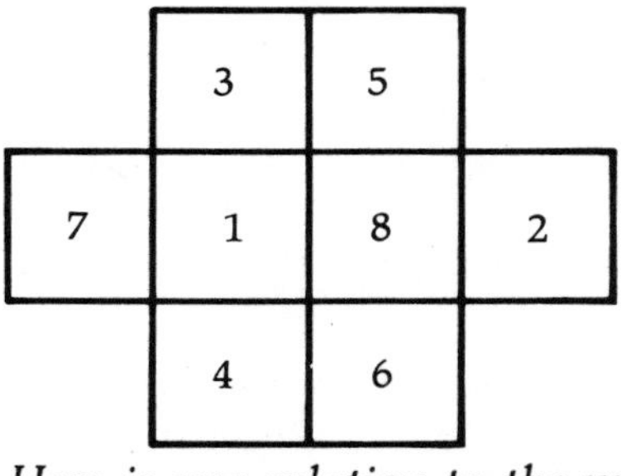

Figure 14. Here is one solution to the problem of the eight boxes. There are others, but all must have 1 and 8 in the centermost boxes.

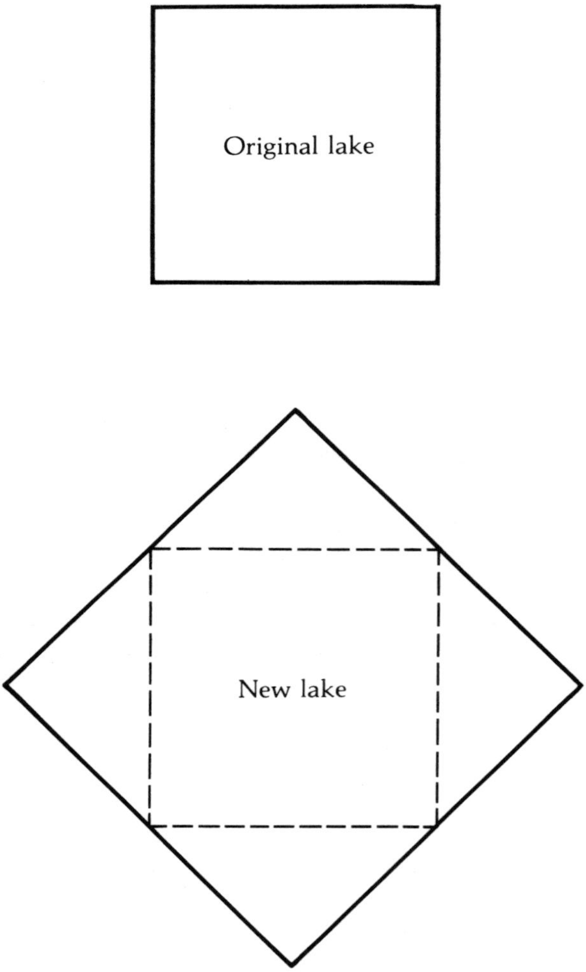

Figure 15. The original lake and the new lake. We must overcome the tendency to make the implicit assumption that the sides of the new lake must be parallel to those of the original lake if we are to achieve a solution.

one with the number 2 in it. Since every number of 1 through 8 other than 1 and 8 has *two* neighbors (e.g., 3 has neighbors 2 and 4), none of those numbers (2, 3, 4, 5, 6, 7) can be in the center. Thus, 1 and 8 *must* be in the center. That observation, in turn, forces 2 and 7 to be in the extreme boxes (leftmost and rightmost). The rest is easy.

3. Figure 15 should be intuitive and self-explanatory. Note that the difficulty for some people is that they never consider rotating the figure. Follow-up: Now that you've seen this, and knowing that the new boundary lines are drawn in at 45-degree angles to the original ones, can you *prove* formally that the new lake's area is indeed exactly double that of the original lake?

4. Figure 16 provides the solution to the problem with the glasses.

Figure 16. Pour the water from the second glass into the fifth glass

Chapter 3

1. By pattern, we'll see that the sum of the first n odd numbers is n^2. Therefore, the sum of the first 50 odds is $50 \times 50 = 2500$. To see the pattern:

one odd number: $1 = 1 = 1 \times 1$
two odd numbers: $1 + 3 = 4 = 2 \times 2$
three odd numbers: $1 + 3 + 5 = 9 = 3 \times 3$
and so on.

2. If you explore the pattern, you find, for one even number, a sum of 2, which is 1×2. For two even numbers, it's $2 + 4 = 6$, which $= 2 \times 3$. For three, it's $2 + 4 + 6 = 12$, which $= 3 \times 4$. Evidently, we can prove, for the first n even numbers, the sum is $n(n + 1)$. Using $n = 100$ gives $100 \times 101 = 10,100$.

3. Here the pattern is "involved" due to the fractions. If you calculate for several terms, you find that the answers are $1/2$ using one term, $2/3$ for two terms, $3/4$ for three terms. We can prove that this pattern does indeed hold for all n where the sum of the first n such terms is $n/(n+1)$. (Challenge: Show this.) Thus, since we had ninety-nine terms, it's $99/100$.

4. For $1/2 + 1/4 + 1/8 + 1/16 + \ldots + 1/4096$, you can discover a similar pattern to get the result $1 - 1/4096$ or $4095/4096$.

5. The key is to break down the squares by sizes. The number of 8×8 squares is 1; of 7×7 is 4; of 6×6 is 9. Note that these numbers of squares are the consecutive perfect squares. So, the answer is $1 + 4 + 9 + 16 + 25 + 36 + 49 + 64$, or 204 squares altogether.

6. For a quadrilateral (polygon of four sides), you can draw one diagonal from one vertex. For a pentagon (or 5-gon), it's two, and it's three for a hexagon. The pattern is that an n-gon has $n - 3$ diagonals emanating from any one vertex. Since adding one more side always produces one extra diagonal, the pattern is genuine and persists.

Hence, for a chiliagon, a polygon of a thousand sides, the number sought is $1000-3=997$.

By a similar process, the number of triangles formed in an n-gon when the $n-3$ diagonals are drawn is $n-2$. For a chiliagon it is therefore 998.

7. The question of the number of open cells boils down to asking the number of perfect squares from 1 to 1000. Since 32 squared is over 1000, but $31\times31 = 961$, the answer is 31 for a jail of 1000 cells.

Chapter 4

1. Player 1 has the natural advantage. He or she should pick 1 on the first turn. Thereafter, whenever player 2 picks x, player 1 should pick $9-x$.

2. This time player 2 has the advantage, and all he or she need do is pick 10 minus whatever player 1 previously picked each time.

3. The moral is to see the diagonal as both a diagonal and as the hypotenuse of a right triangle. This allows the bridge needed. If a side is denoted s, then, by the Pythagorean theorem, $s^2+s^2=60^2=3600$. But then s^2 alone $= 1800$, and this is also the area (another nice bridge). Thus area $= 1800$ cm^2. Note that there is no need to find the value of s! See Figure 17.

4. We must find the area of the quarter-circle and that of the rectangle, and then subtract. The rectangle has an area of $6 \times 8 = 48$. The quarter-circle's is $(1/4)\,\pi r^2$. But what is the radius r? If you look at the rectangle, you'll see that one of the diagonals is a radius. But the diagonals of a rectangle are equal in length. So, by the Pythagorean theorem, $6^2 + 8^2 = r^2$. Solving gives $r = 10$. So,

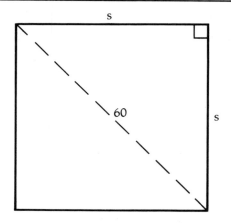

Figure 17. Area and the Pythagorean Theorem are frequently intertwined, as in the question involving the area of a square whose diagonal is 60.

the quarter-circle has area 25π, and thus, the required area is $25\pi - 48$. See Figure 18.   ✓

5. Let t = the time in years needed for the populations to be equal. When that happens, $1600 + 120t = 4200 - 80t$. Solving, we get $200t = 2600$, so t = 13 years.

(A faster approach: Each year, the populations come 200 people closer. They are initially 2600 apart. Dividing 2600 by 200 produces 13.)

Hence, each village has 3,160 inhabitants 13 years later, for a combined population of 6,320.

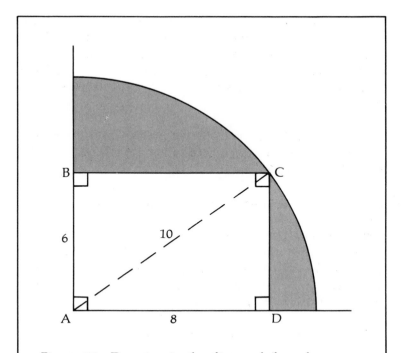

Figure 18. *Drawing in the diagonal that also serves as a radius builds the bridge needed here.*

Chapter 5

1. Use the formula d = rt (distance = rate × time) in the form t = d/r to obtain the times for the 400 miles: 1/4 hour, 1/3 hour, 1/2 hour, and 1 hour, respectively. The total time is therefore the sum 1/4 + 1/3 + 1/2 + 1 = 3/12 + 4/12 + 6/12 + 12/12 = 25/12 hours. Hence, the plane's average speed is 400/(25/12) = 400 × 12/25 = 192 kilometers per hour.

2. $(1/10)/(3/4)$, which equals $(1/10) \times (4/3) = 2/15$. This question's answer has a nice interpretation: What part of three-quarters of a dollar is a dime? Since a dime is equivalent to two nickels, and three quarters to fifteen nickels, the answer is two nickels over fifteen nickels, or our $2/15$ answer. ✓

3. (C) 25%. If the item costs x originally, after the reduction it costs 0.8x. To get back to x, we must add 0.2x. The part change is $0.2x/0.8x = 1/4 = 25\%$.

4. The correct answer is *not* $5 to Mary, $3 to Dick. Let's see why not. Mary brought five bottles, or $15 worth. However, she consumed $8 worth. Hence, she contributed $7 more than she consumed. Dick brought $9 worth and consumed $8 worth, so he is entitled to $1. The error made by those who say $5 and $3 is in failing to account for personal consumption.

5. The sum of the six numbers averaging 8 is 48, as is the sum of the eighty numbers averaging 6. There are therefore fourteen numbers, all of which have a sum of 96. Hence, the average is $96/14 = 48/7$, or 6 6/7. ✓

Chapter 6

1. $2 in currency can be decomposed into pennies, nickels, and dimes in $1 + 3 + 5 + \ldots + 41$ ways, as in the example. Since we know the sum of the first n odd numbers, with n = 21 in this case, the answer is $21 \times 21 = 441$.

2. Each "broken line" in Figure 19 contains an odd number of dots. Do you see how you get a square showing, *without adding*, $1 + 3 + 5 + 7 + 9 + 11 + 13 + 15 + 17 + 19 = 10^2 = 100$?

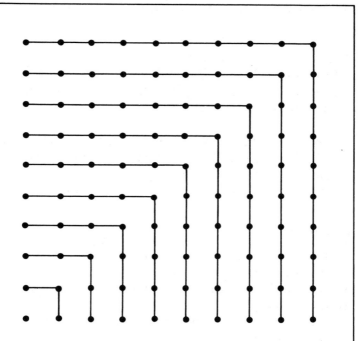

Figure 19. Each broken line contains an odd number of dots, forming the square and illustrating that the first ten consecutive odd numbers add to $10 \times 10 = 100$.

Chapter 7

1. 1×6 (1 times 6).

2. Use three to form an equilateral triangle. Now add the other three to form a pyramidlike structure—a tetrahedron, to be precise. (Nobody said the matchsticks all had to lie in the same plane! Watch those implicit assumptions!)

3. Open the door and walk out! (Nobody said the door was locked!)

4. If PQ = 1 centimeter, we still don't have enough information. Ditto if QR = 2 centimeters. However, if we have both of these lengths given, then RS will obviously be larger than PQ.

5. For x<0, 5+x² > 5−x². This is true, in fact, as long as x isn't zero; i.e., it is not necessary that x always be negative (or that x always be positive, for that matter). As long as x is positive or negative, the result holds.

Chapter 8

1. The sum of three consecutive natural numbers is always divisible by: (A) 3 only. We can see that the answer can't be 5 only, 3 and 5, or 7 only, from the example using 1 + 3 + 5 = 9.

How do we know the answer is (A) 3 only, and not (E) none of these?

We could use many more examples to persuade us, but there is an easy short proof available. For instance, if the middle number of the three numbers is x, then the smallest is x−1 and the largest is x+1. The sum of the three numbers is 3x, making it a multiple of 3.

Lastly, by varying x, we can show that the sum need not be a multiple of any other particular prescribed number.

2. Here's one way. Write out the numbers 1 to 100: 1 + 2 + 3 + . . . + 98 + 99 + 100. Now couple as

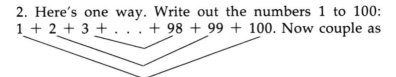

indicated.

There are 50 pairs of numbers indicated, and each has sum = 101. So, the sum = 50 × 101 = 5050.

There are other approaches to this, but note that the key ingredient needed is that the numbers be in an arithmetic sequence. That is, there must be a constant difference between consecutive terms. For the natural numbers, that difference is 1; for odd numbers, it's 2.

3. Each vertex can be connected to every other vertex except itself and the two vertices adjacent to it. Hence, $n-3$ diagonals, one to each of the n vertices other than the three exceptions.

Chapter 9

1. If the length is L, then $L^2 + (5/4)^2 = (13/4)^2$. Thus, $L^2 = (169-25)/16 = 144/16 = 9$, so $L = 3$.

2. Draw the diagram first, as in Figure 20. Then draw in the other segments shown to form a right triangle of legs

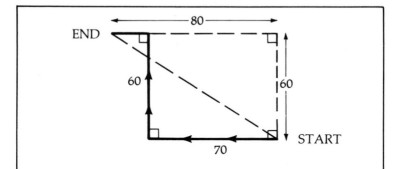

Figure 20. The solid lines indicate the original route, but the dashed one drawn in produces the distance between start and finish (as though a direct path were available). The Pythagorean Theorem works best in such a problem, which is easier if you note that the triangle is similar to a 3:4:5 one.

60 and 80. By the Pythagorean theorem, we can get that the direct line path is 100 kilometers long (that is, the hypotenuse is 100). Of course, you can get this faster by noting that the legs have a 3:4 ratio, so the hypotenuse should come from the 3:4:5 triangle, except that each number here is 20 times as large ($60 = 20 \times 3$, $80 = 20 \times 4$, so the third side $= 20 \times 5 = 100$).

3. The average is $(63 + 63)/16 = 126/16 = 63/8$ or (B) 7 7/8. This time the answers are "closer together" relatively speaking, so it is more difficult to eliminate choices. Elimination and taking shortcuts involving estimating work best when the answers are relatively far apart.

Chapter 10

1. How can the sum from 1 to 100 be only 50?

2. How can the sum of whole numbers not be a whole number?

3. How can a sum of positives be negative?

4. A triangle with sides 5.5, 5.5, and 14 cannot possibly exist. (Why not?)

Chapter 11

1. All the paths are of the same length, basically because the opposite sides of a rectangle have the same length.

2. Let $u=x^2$. We want to maximize $10x^2 - 20x^4 = 10u - 20u^2$. It is well known that the extreme value of a quadratic au^2+bu+c occurs when $u = -b/2a$. Here,

a$=-20$ and b$=10$. $\therefore$ u$=-10/2(-20)=1/4$. (Thus, x $= \pm$ 1/2, but we can work with u.) The maximum value is then $10(1/4) - 20(1/4)^2 = 2.5 - 1.25 = 1.25$ or 1 1/4 or 5/4. There's no minimum, however.

3. Official solution follows:
Since $0 < p \le x \le 15$, then $|x - p| = x - p$, $|x - 15| = 15 - x$, and $|x - (p + 15)| = p + 15 - x$. Thus

$$f(x) = (x-p) + (15-x) + (p + 15 - x) = 30 - x.$$

It follows that f(x) is least when x is greatest, and that the answer is 15.

4. Official solution follows:
The answer is 20. Here are the details.

Substitute to simplify. Several choices work well; the following substitution, which eliminates the radical immediately, is perhaps best. Define u to be the non-negative number such that $u^2 = x^2 + 18x + 45$. (There is such a u, for if $x^2 + 18x + 45$ were negative, the right-hand side of the original equation would be undefined.) So

$$u^2 - 15 = 2\sqrt{u^2} = 2u \text{ (since } u \ge 0),$$
$$u^2 - 2u - 15 = 0,$$
$$(u - 5)(u + 3) = 0.$$

Since $u \ge 0$, we have u $=$ 5. That is, x is a solution of the original equation iff (if and only if) $x^2 + 18x + 45 = 5^2$, that is, iff $x^2 + 18x + 20 = 0$. Both solutions to this last equation are real (why?) and their product is the constant term, 20. (Note: By being careful about the sign of u and by using iff-arguments we have avoided introducing any extraneous roots for x.)

5. If each side of the square has length s, then the diagonal, which is also the hypotenuse of a right triangle,

has length $s\sqrt{2}$, which is about 1.4s. The percentage less is therefore

$$\frac{\text{amount less}}{\text{longer amount}} \times 100\% = \frac{2-1.4}{2} \times 100\%$$

$$= 30\% \quad \text{(approximately)}.$$

FOR FURTHER READING

There are many fine books on problem solving, as well as mathematics publications, and other materials worth looking into.

Best bets: Check your library for any of the problem solving books by George Polya. If you're interested in recreational mathematics, seek out the books of Martin Gardner, a few of which are listed below.

Get involved with problem solving in at least one of the journals featuring a problem section. Ask your teacher or librarian if the school or library can order such collegiate publications as *The AMATYC Review, Crux Mathematicorum, Mathematics Magazine, The College Mathematics Journal, Pi Mu Epsilon Journal, The Pentagon, School Science and Mathematics,* and *The Journal of Recreational Mathematics.*

Also look into publications of the National Council of Teachers of Mathematics, 1906 Association Drive, Reston, VA 22091. NCTM is more devoted to junior and senior high school mathematics, and this may be a more appropriate place to start for most readers.

For high school and collegiate material, contact the Mathematical Association of America, 1529 Eighteenth St., N.W., Washington, DC 20036. The MAA produces books of past contests and other books of interest to mathematicians or those aspiring to learn mathematics.

For information on contests of the Committee on American Mathematics Competitions, contact the MAA, or better, contact its present Executive Director, Dr. Walter Mientka, Department of Mathematics and Statistics, University of Nebraska, Lincoln, NE 68588-0322.

One recent article of interest at the collegiate level, illustrating the diverse approaches to problem solving (as applied to just one problem), appeared in the November 1985 *College Mathematics Journal*. See Loren C. Larson's "A Discrete Look at $1 + 2 + \ldots + n$" (pages 369-382). Professor Larson is also a problem department editor and the editor of a book, *Problem Solving Through Problems*, which is essentially a compilation of problems in collegiate mathematics.

Eventually, any true problem solver will become interested in problem posing. For those interested in this flip side of the coin, I recommend the book *The Art of Problem Posing* by Stephen I. Brown and Marion I. Walter. Professors Brown and Walter have produced many fine contributions to problem-solving theory.

Following is a list of books, including the above titles, for further reading. It is at best a start, for a complete list of useful materials would fill an entire book.

Averbach, Bonnie, and Chein, Orin. *Mathematics: Problem Solving Through Recreational Mathematics*. W.H. Freeman, 1980.

Brown, Stephen I., and Marion I. Walter. *The Art of Problem Posing*. Franklin Institute Press, 1983. This book is now available only through Lawrence Earlbaum Associates, 365 Broadway, Hillsdale, N.J. 07642. This publisher also produces other books on teaching and learning problem solving.

Dalton, Leroy C., and Henry D. Snyder, eds. *Topics for Mathematics Clubs*. National Council of Teachers of Mathematics, 1973.

Ecker, Michael W. "Recreational Applications of Elementary Number Theory." *The Pentagon*, January 1982.

Gardner, Martin. *Aha! Gotcha: Paradoxes to Puzzle and Delight.* W.H. Freeman, 1982.   — ✓

_____. *Mathematical Carnival.* Knopf, 1965.

_____. *Mathematics, Magic, and Mystery.* Dover, 1956. This publisher is a supplier of nice, inexpensive books on mathematics and recreations.

Honsberger, Ross. *Ingenuity in Mathematics.* The Mathematical Association of America, 1970.

Krulik, Stephen, ed. *Problem Solving in School Mathematics* (1980 Yearbook). National Council of Teachers of Mathematics, 1980.

Larson, Loren C., ed. *Problem Solving Through Problems.* Springer-Verlag, 1983.

Lewis, David B. *Eureka! Math Fun from Many Angles.* Putnam, 1983. This book's distinction is more with its author than the recreations; the author wrote it while in high school.

Polya, George. *How to Solve It.* Princeton University Press, 1945.

_____. *Mathematical Discovery: On Understanding, Learning, and Teaching Problem Solving.* John Wiley & Sons, 1962.

Schoenfeld, Alan H. *Problem Solving in the Mathematics Curriculum.* The Mathematical Association of America, 1983. Schoenfeld's work contains at least seventy pages of information on problem-solving resources, and is highly recommended on the strength of its bibliography alone, therefore. The first half of the book contains valuable problem information apart from the lengthy bibliography, too.

INDEX

Gardner, Martin, 121, 123

Honsberger, Ross, 123
How to Solve It (Polya), 123

Implicit assumptions,
    dangers of, 56–57
    algebraic example, 59
    distance, rate and
        time problem, 47,
        48
    geometric example,
        57–59, *57, 58*
    sample problems and
        answers, 16, 56,
        59–60, 115–16
Ingenuity in Mathematics
    (Honsberger), 123

Jailer problem, 31–32, *33*
Journals on problem solv-
    ing, 121, 122

Krulik, Stephen, 123

Larson, Loren C., 122,
    123
Lewis, David B., 123
Lists of possibilities
    notations in, 50–51
    organization in, 50
    patterns in, 52–53
    sample problems and
        answers, 54–55,
        114, *115*

suggestive nature in
    terms of a solution,
    52–53

Math ability, 15–16
Math clubs, 25, 104
Math contests
    anxiety, dealing with,
        104–5
    Committee on Ameri-
        can Mathematics
        competitions, 20,
        21, 22–24
    competitive nature
        of, 18
    conventional exams,
        comparison with,
        24–25
    formats of, 23, 106
    guessing at answers,
        23, 24, 106
    instructions for, 18–
        19
    junior college level
        exams, 19, 22–23
    local and regional ex-
        ams, 19
    no-lose nature of,
        25–26
    olympiads, 19, 22,
        23–24
    participation prere-
        quisites, 15–16
    preparation for, 25,
        104–6
    prizes, 20, 24